Bernad Kurx

THE GREEK TRADITION

THE GREEK TRADITION

ESSAYS IN THE RECONSTRUCTION OF ANCIENT THOUGHT

BY

J. A. K. THOMSON

WITH A PREFACE BY PROF. GILBERT MURRAY

PAUL P. APPEL, *Publisher*

MAMARONECK, N.Y.

1971

Originally Published 1915
Reprinted 1971

Published by PAUL P. APPEL
By Arrangement With
GEORGE ALLEN & UNWIN LTD.

Library of Congress Catalog Card Number—70-162501
ISBN 911858-23-7

Let all men judge, who is it can deny
That the rich crown of old Humanity
Is still your birthright? and was ne'er let down
From heaven for rule of beasts' lives, but your own?

CHAPMAN.

INTRODUCTION

WHEN Mr. Thomson's fine Studies in the Odyssey appeared, I happened to notice one solemn reviewer who, after four lines of earnest misdescription, concluded by expressing his grief that any University had published such a book. It should have been strangled unborn and its author effectually silenced. Meditating on the point of view disclosed, I remembered that exactly the same thing had been said about one of my own early books. And, on further reflection, I recalled at least three other scholars, now occupying University Chairs or similar positions, whose early writings were welcomed in the same way.

There is nothing odd in this. It is only one more reminder to us old and established scholars to keep our minds as alert as we can, and not grow stiff and deaf in our favourite orthodoxies. But the incident made me try to think why I had derived so much pleasure and instruction from a book which other students appeared whole-heartedly to despise.

I think the reason probably lies in a certain divergence of view about the proper aims of scholarship. When a scholar prepares to comment upon an ancient poem—say an Ode of Pindar—he may, for instance, find out from the lexica the received translations of all the words, analyse the syntax, identify the dialectical forms, tabulate the comments of the scholia and make a scheme of the metre ; he may, with luck, collect definite evidence of the date at which the Ode was performed. So far he will be on what is called 'safe ground.' It is not in the least safe really ; for the lexicon interpretation will probably be inadequate, the syntax of a particular passage may have some subtlety of its own which escapes the broad rule, the scholia will be confused or, more important still, will not have sufficient command of exegetical language to say what they mean, and so on. But it is safe in the sense that, if he is challenged, he can give "chapter and verse" for all his statements. And of course he will have done valuable work.

Yet he will not yet have asked himself the two questions that matter most : What does this poem mean ? and What is there fine about it ? Still less will he have asked a third question : How did it come to be what it is ?

Now these questions are rather like the great problems of philosophy. Philosophers tell us that, though we may never raise those problems or even know of their existence, we cannot help consciously or unconsciously answering them. I believe there are scholars who, by great self-restraint, inhibit their natural curiosity and try their best to avoid asking any question whose answer does not admit of what they would call proof. But they do not really succeed. All that happens is that since these questions cannot be 'counted' in examinations and since they demand faculties which the ordinary routine of a scholar's or teacher's life does not specially cultivate, they answer them carelessly or irritably. They treat them as trifles and interruptions. And when they find a scholar, like Mr. Thomson, who is almost entirely occupied with such subjects, they are bewildered. They expect him to be answering their questions, whereas he is really answering his own. And they read, skipping and skipping and wondering when the point is coming, and in the end do not see what it was all about; they only know that they violently disagree with, say, a footnote on p. 1000.

Now of late there has been an interesting change of emphasis in the study of Greek, a change, we may say, from morphology towards semantics: from the study of forms towards the study of meanings. Of course neither side can be neglected with impunity. But from the semantic point of view the central fact to grasp is that to understand Greek literature you must be able to understand literature, and that you cannot understand literature without using your imagination. Your imagination is, of course, faulty and liable to mislead —just like your other faculties. You can never arrive at certain and complete knowledge of what Aeschylus had in his mind when he composed a particular passage. But, unless you prefer to give up trying to understand anything at all, the only help is to train your imagination, widen its range and improve its sensitiveness, and by increased knowledge make it a better instrument for approaching the truth.

Of course a weak or lazy or irresponsible imagination is no use at all. Indeed the quality on whose usefulness I am insisting might perhaps be called power of analysis rather than merely imagination. It is the power and the practice of thinking out and realizing as much as possible the facts with which one deals, never using them merely like counters or algebraical formulae, nor again translating them carelessly into the first " modern equivalent" that comes to hand. I have often marvelled at the misunderstandings of Athenian history which come from treating Cleon straight off as a modern Radical and Aristophanes as a Tory. They illustrate the value of Moritz Haupt's oracular saying : "Never translate ; translation is the death of understanding." Of course you must translate some time, but the great thing is not to translate too soon—to think in Greek terms as long as you can, and use, in your effort at understanding, Greek ideas and ways of thought. If we want to understand Cleon, let us start with " the most violent of the citizens" and proceed to collect the rest of the evidence about him. If we want to understand " Komodia " or to grasp Heracles as a " komic " hero, let us start by grasping the root idea of the ancient " Komos." Then the way will become clear—so clear that we shall probably forget how much we owe to Mr. Thomson for pointing it out. It will never be clear if we start from Shakespeare and Meredith's *Essay on Comedy.*

If a scholar attempts to understand his subject with this degree of thoroughness ; if he tries really to feel the meaning and the connotations of every important word, if he faces each familiar thought or practice until it seems strange and then tries to trace the path by which such strange things became natural and in-evitable ; then, if he has the requisite equipment of learning and imagination and sensitiveness, he is sure to produce work of real beauty and value, and equally sure to leave much of his work uncertain and inconclusive and his full purpose unachieved. So that some readers will certainly delight in him, while some no doubt will continue simply to wonder why such books should be written and printed.

GILBERT MURRAY.

CONTENTS

ON AN OLD MAP

I HAVE been looking at an *Orbis Terrarum ad Mentem
Herodoti* or Map of the Earth according to Herodotus.
It is roughly circular in shape, with some faint resemblance to a human skull facing west. Deep into it,
almost through it, penetrates a great breach of waters
in a diminishing series of enormous lakes, the Mediterranean with the Aegean, the Black Sea, and the Palus
Maeotis or Sea of Azov. East of the Black Sea is
shown the landlocked Caspian ; it looks about the
size of the Sea of Azov. The Mediterranean countries
are just recognizable. But Asia Minor is grotesquely
out of proportion. It is almost fan-shaped, with the
Aegean coast representing the outspread edge of the fan.
The Nile forms two sides of a square, and rises
apparently somewhere about Lake Chad. The Danube
rises apparently in the Pyrenees. The outer rims
of the *Orbis* fade away vaguely into uncharted seas
and unexplored wildernesses tenanted in the north
by ' Hyperboreans ' and ' Arimaspeans ', in the west by
' Celts ', in the south by ' Ethiopians ' and again by
' Long-lived Ethiopians '. The east is quite frankly
Deserta Incognita, the Unknown. The whole looks
rather like a sketch of the Mediterranean World made
by a child from memory upon a round piece of
paper.

Yet what a wonderful thing is the mere possibility of such a map! Herodotus wrote in an age when science had just come into existence, and exact scientific instruments did not exist at all. He had been a great traveller, a great hearer of travellers' tales. He had also, to guide him, the maps of earlier geographers, *Periodoi Gês* they were called, 'The Way round the World'. But the maps excite his ridicule; 'I laugh when I see them', he says. Conceive the difficulty in those days of forming an adequate notion of the shapes of foreign countries or even of your own country. Suppose you had never seen a map except of the kind that made even Herodotus laugh, and then imagine the sketch you would make of the British Isles from mere hearsay and the witness of your own eyes. Herodotus had to do something like that. He had to travel without a theodolite, without a telescope, without a compass. He had to carry distances and natural features in his head. When he went to sea he must enter a little wooden craft, which was helpless in a current, helpless when the stars were hidden of nights, helpless in a high wind, helpless (save for the oars) in no wind at all. He had to piece out his own observations with the confused and sometimes lying stories of Greek sailors and half-breed dragomans. Yet out of his book modern geographers can construct a quite plausible map of Southern Europe. It is really very wonderful.

To the average Greek of Herodotus' time and even later such a map was an almost incredible curiosity. Only a subtle Ionian would possess such a thing. When Aristagoras the tyrant of Miletus came to Sparta to ask for help against the Persian, he brought a map with him, 'a bronze tablet on which was cut the Circle of all the Lands, with every sea, and all the rivers'. He explained it all to the Spartan king Cleomenes. "Here are the Ionians, and next them the Lydians, who live in a good land and have store of silver. . . . Here are the Phrygians, the easterly neighbours of the Lydians, with more sheep and finer harvests than any other people I know. Next to the Phrygians come the Cappadocians, whom we call the Syrians. *Their* neighbours are the Cilicians, whose country stretches down to the sea *here*, in which lies the island of Cyprus *there*. . . ." So Aristagoras proceeded, says Herodotus, pointing to the places as he mentioned them. The Spartan was impressed but puzzled. Aristagoras tried an appeal to his cupidity. He told of Susa the capital of the Great King, where the royal treasures were stored. "Take that city, and you rival Zeus in wealth!" And the 'barbarians' are really great cowards. "The way they fight is like this—bows and arrows and a little spear! They go into battle in trousers and mitres! So easy are they to overcome!" Cleomenes, however, wanted a little time to think; he was a Spartan. He would give his answer at the end of two days. His first question, when they met again, showed that he had been thinking hard. He asked how many days' journey it was from the coast of Ionia to Susa. "Three months" was the incautious answer. "Milesian stranger, get you gone from Sparta before sunset! A hard request is this of yours to Lacedaemonians, expecting them to perform a three months' journey from the sea!" Cleomenes had thought it might take as many days. Everything had looked so little on the map.

Cleomenes to be sure was a Spartan, and lived two generations before Herodotus. But one suspects that the geography of the average country-bred Athenian in the great age of Pericles was quite as hazy as that of Cleomenes, an able man, who had led armies up and down Greece and knew at least the military value of topography. There is a laughable little scene in the *Clouds* of Aristophanes which shows us how an old-fashioned Athenian regarded a map. Strepsiades is admiring the wonders of Socrates' academy for young philosophers. A disciple points out a *Periodos Gês*, like that exhibited by Aristagoras but doubtless greatly improved. Strepsiades is shown Athens—" I don't believe you ", he interrupts, " I don't see the jury-courts sitting ",—Attica, the interminable island of Euboea. " Where is Sparta ? " he asks eagerly. The disciple indicates it. " So near! You should apply your whole mind to the problem of removing it quite a long distance away from us." " But that is impossible." " Very well, you'll regret it, that's all." Strepsiades is a character in a play, and a buffoon at that ; but he is typical. He is the 'ironical' man who is not such a fool as he looks. He reverses in his own favour the epigram, so full of human wisdom in its apparent simplicity, *The Milesians are not stupid, but they behave as if they were.* I gather from this scene that maps were moderately familiar to Aristophanes' audiences, but that old people were puzzled to death by them. As for *making* a map, only a Wise Man, a Sophist, could do that !

However disposed Herodotus was to laugh at the maps of the Ionians, he certainly made use of them. As a matter of fact no one sits down to make an original map. It would be a foolish waste of time, even if one had the knowledge to do it. At best the cartographer makes detailed improvements in the existing maps. The most modern and scientific is simply the Tablet of Aristagoras improved out of all recognition. We know that considerable portions of the History of Herodotus are based upon the *Logos* of his great predecessor, Hecataeus of Miletus, and we have good reason for thinking that this Logos was in effect 'what Hecataeus said' about the map of Anaximander. Anaximander was a fellow-citizen, a great genius with a wonderful gift of scientific imagination. To fix his conception of the universe in its superficial appearance, he constructed a map, the first of which we hear. What it was like we can only guess. But a careful reading of Herodotus has made it possible to detect what look like certain guiding principles in these first rudimentary *Periodoi*. Anaximander availed himself of two long straight lines, one natural and the other artificial, which served in their way for lines of longitude and latitude. The natural line was formed by the courses of the Danube and the Nile, which were supposed to flow from north to south and south to north respectively, and so to make one straight line interrupted by the Levant and the Aegean. The artificial line was the great Royal Road of the Persian Empire between Sardis and Susa. Every part of the map was made symmetrical with some other part, and the whole was surrounded by the River Ocean, drawn, Herodotus says, 'as if with a pair of compasses'.

But was Anaximander's really the first map? The first scientific map it no doubt was, making 'Asia', that

is practically what we call Asia Minor, 'just equal to
Europe' according to a definite scientific hypothesis.
But there may quite probably have been before Anaximander an ancient traditional *Periplus* or Mariners'
Guide roughly indicating the outlines of the seas known
to Greek sailors, and marking their dangers and the
places near the coast where fresh water was procurable.
M. Victor Bérard in his book on the Phoenicians and
the *Odyssey* has tried to shew that the wanderings of
Odysseus are, as it were, an imaginative rendering of
such a *Periplus*. It is not in itself an impossible theory ;
there is in fact a great deal to be said in its favour.
But when M. Bérard thinks of the Phoenicians as the
original authors of his traditional *Periplus*, which the
Greeks borrowed and translated, and so handed down
to the long and varied line of their successors in the
command of the seas, until it has become embodied at
last in the *Mediterranean Pilot* issued by the British
Admiralty—when Bérard says this, certain old familiar
doubts begin to assail us. Those Phoenicians! How
often we have followed their stern-lights into impossible
shoals of speculation! Indeed, since Bérard wrote his
book not so many years ago, discoveries have been
made which have quite dissolved the mirage of a great
Phoenician empire of the seas. There was such an
empire in prehistoric times. But it did not belong to
Palestine ; it belonged to Crete. It has been thought
that the rapid expansion of the Phoenician sea-power
about 1000 B.C. was due to an infusion of Cretan influences, and that the Philistines, who may have brought
these influences, came, if not from Crete, at any rate
from a land with the Old Cretan or, as scholars say,
'Minoan' civilization. On this view, which is now

perhaps generally accepted, the *Periplus* which the Phoenicians in Bérard's opinion possessed may well have been borrowed from Crete. But we need not really trouble about that. What we are concerned with is the Ionian *Periplus*, which demonstrably did exist. We may dismiss the theory that it was based upon a Phoenician predecessor. But was it not perhaps based upon a Cretan one?

We could better estimate the probability of this, if we knew for certain who the Ionians were. One thing is certain: whatever their racial affinities, the first settlers in Ionia were imbued with the 'Minoan' culture. And since they settled in the heart of the Cretan sea-empire of the Aegean, we may reasonably infer that they inherited, along with the 'Minoan' civilization in general, something of the sea-lore (not of course necessarily incorporated in any actual in-scribed *Periplus*) which enabled the Cretan ships to voyage so boldly and so far.

The point is worth considering. Herodotus tells us that the navy of Minos, the typical ruler of 'Minoan' Crete, was manned from the pre-Greek population of the Aegean islands. That population was never extermi-nated, it survived in the Carians of historical times. Now it was exactly among these Carians that the Ionians settled. That there was a large Carian element (Carians with some tincture of the 'Minoan' culture) in the Ionians of history is regarded as certain. Does it not seem on the whole a very probable thing that the traditional lore of that old seafaring population was preserved a long time after the fall of the Cretan power? This hypothesis at least helps to explain the really startling phenomenon of the Greek Colonization.

The true character of that very wonderful movement is obscured for us by a cloud of legends ; while the few solid facts which do emerge have passed through the simplifying and dramatizing processes of the popular imagination. Even the picture suggested by modern historians—Greek navigators sailing along an unknown coast on the look out for a likely site for some prosperous new city—is really too Utopian. No ; the colonists went where trade was doing. If you consult a map you will see that the great Greek colonies were planted as a rule at the ends of immemorial trade-routes. Marseille is at the bottom of the Rhone valley. Cyrene was the terminus of the caravan route from the Oasis of Siwah. Sinope was the end of a commercial road from Boghaz-Keui, the ancient capital of the Hittites. These great trading stations were not discovered by the Greeks. They had been exploited long before. There is accumulating evidence that ' Minoan' goods travelled over a region nearly coextensive with the Greek colonial empire. If you read with some care Herodotus' account of the ' founding' of Cyrene, you will easily see that the advice to found it was based upon knowledge which could never have been snatched up by a storm-stressed merchantman. The advice came from Delphi. Now, there are two things to remark about that. The first is that in ancient times the priests are the great preservers of traditional lore. The second is that the Delphian Oracle in the prevalent tradition was instituted by Cretans. There can be very little doubt that the Old Cretans knew the Cyrenaica, just as they knew much remoter lands like South Italy and Sicily and Spain. Even Marseille (Massalia) and Aleria, the Greek colony in Corsica, may be Cretan names.

May we therefore assume that the Greek colonial empire—the term is used colloquially—was an attempt to reconstitute the great colonial or trading system of Old Crete ruined by the irruption of the Hellenes? There is this to be said. The Greeks themselves were aware that King Minos was the founder of the first *Thalassocracy* or Sea-Control. Thucydides implies that the Athenian naval power maintained the place once held by the ships of Crete. An ancient document has been extracted from Diodorus and Eusebius which gives a list of the 'Thalassocrats' from the Fall of Troy to the founding of the Athenian League. Such a list clearly assumes that the command of the sea was not a thing of 'to-day or yesterday'. Ultimately, as Thucydides understood, the Thalassocracy went back to Minos. Consider the interest of this for the student of Greek literature. The ancient epic poetry of Greece is full of a marvellous, fantastic geography. Odysseus sails to a land where men live on " a flowery food " that steeps their minds in a strange forgetfulness, to a sea where the rocks float and clash, to a land where night never falls. Jason voyages to the Land of the Golden Fleece. Is it all fable? Scholars used to say that the localization of the Land of the Golden Fleece in Colchis at the eastern corner of the Black Sea must be later than the voyages of the Milesians along the northern coast of Anatolia. This assumes that the Greeks had never even heard of Colchis before Ionian ships went there. I believe they had heard of it. There was a primitive trade-route between the Caspian and the Black Sea through a broad deep valley in the Caucasus. By that channel flows to-day the trade between Baku and Batum. Homer knew of 'far-off

Alybe, where silver is born', somewhere perhaps in the neighbourhood of Erzrum. 'Minoan' ships may have gone for silver to the mouth of the Phasis before Ionia was colonized at all.

The Argonauts also visited Cyrene. Remember that tradition persistently calls them 'Minyans', that is, some scholars would say, 'Minoans'. They had at any rate the 'Minoan' civilization. Why must we assume that the visit to Cyrene is an episode added after the 'foundation' of the Greek town by the Theraeans? That is the 'safe' theory. But what is the use of a safe theory if it is incredible? Again, Jason and his men sail up the Danube and down the 'Eridanus'. Well, the cautious scholar insists, that at least never happened! It never happened, certainly. But if 'Minoan' merchants heard vague rumours that it was actually possible to ship goods up the Danube and down the Rhine or the Rhone; if goods did as a matter of fact come to them in that way; would not this piece of real experience help to project the legend? How did Homer know that there was a land of the midnight sun, and a northern land of Cimmerian darkness?

As it falls out, we are able to test the validity of one of these stories, the strangest, the most incredible-seeming of them all. It concerns the Hyperboreans. They come very early into Greek literature. 'Hesiod has spoken about them, and Homer also in the *Epigoni*, if Homer is the real author of the *Epigoni*.' But it is the people of Delos, Herodotus proceeds, who have most to tell us about the Hyperboreans, and what they say is this. Certain offerings wrapped in wheaten straw were carried from the land of the Hyperboreans into Scythia. The Scythians passed them on to their next neighbours; and so from tribe to tribe the offerings were borne right down to the head of the Adriatic, and thence south-east to Dodona. From Dodona the sacred messengers struck right across Greece, emerging on the Malian Gulf in Locris. From Locris they crossed to Euboea, where city received them from city until they came to Carystus at the southern extremity of the island. The Carystians convoyed them to the island of Tenos, and the Tenians to Delos. Pausanias, who lived in the time of the Antonines but was nevertheless able to secure a great harvest of extremely ancient temple-legends, gives an entirely different route. In his account the sacred things come by way of the Arimaspeans and the Issedones to Sinope, on the southern shore of the Black Sea, and from Sinope arrive at last at Prasiae in Attica. If the accounts of Herodotus and Pausanias are collated, it will be seen that the Hyperboreans are most naturally placed somewhere in Central Asia. One very learned ethnologist actually thinks of the Chinese. The Greeks themselves had nothing but fables to tell of them. They were an idyllic people, crimeless vegetarians, living somewhere 'beyond the north wind' or, as some conjectured, in the extreme west. 'Neither on shipboard nor yet afoot', says Pindar, 'canst thou find to the Assembly of the Hyperboreans the wondrous way.'

After this it is certainly surprising to discover that the Hyperboreans were a real people. The name was derived by the Greeks themselves from *hyper* and *Boreas*, and understood to mean the dwellers 'beyond the north wind'. It is really a North-Greek word and signifies 'carriers' or 'carriers beyond' or 'across'. Strictly speaking, it is inaccurately applied to the people who first started those 'offerings wrapped in wheaten straw' upon their wondrous way ; it properly belongs to the sacrosanct envoys who bore them from place to place. The Greeks in historical times did not know the true name of the people, nor where they dwelt, nor anything about them except this, that they got their offerings every year. The Greek imagination was naturally touched and wove a cocoon of legends about the one little fact it possessed. Herodotus mentions two Hyperborean maidens 'Hyperoche' and 'Laodice', who were buried in or near 'the precinct of Artemis' at Delos, and another, earlier pair, 'Argê' and 'Opis', who were buried 'behind the Artemisium'. Excavation has brought to light in Delos traces of an early 'Minoan' settlement; a wonderful *Terrace of Lions*, for example, making one think of the primitive 'Lion Goddess' of the Aegean lands. It may very well be that 'Artemis' of Delos is but the old goddess with a Greek name, and that in 'Minoan' times the offerings of the Hyperboreans were really sent to her rather than to Apollo, who came more and more to usurp her ancient prerogatives. At any rate the holy things were sent, and from a very remote period. The traditions prove nothing else, but they prove that. They must have been sent by somebody.

These are vague and distant memories. More clear and traceable is the effect upon geographical knowledge of the great colonization era. At first it is best seen in poetry, for as yet the non-literary records hardly count, and there was no prose literature at all. The coming of the new knowledge is excellently illustrated in the epic of Heracles. The *Heracleia*, as it was called, was a traditional poem. That is to say, the original *Heracleia*, which seems to have been put together in the island of Rhodes, was taken up, developed, extended, written over again, by a series of poets. We hear of three before Herodotus' time: Peisinous of Rhodes, Pisander of Rhodes, Panyassis of Halicarnassus, who was the uncle of Herodotus. That historian evidently knows his *Heracleia* well, although whether it was his uncle's version he went by is another matter. It did not prevent him from doing a little research on his own account into the origins of Heracles, with results which were certainly not orthodox. In the mind of every Greek, however, orthodox or not, Heracles was the embodiment of *Niké*, successful effort. Thus, naturally enough, his achievements to a great extent reflect the achievements of the race. He is the representative of Greek colonial enterprise, and so his adventures take him to the remotest points attained by venturous Greek ships and traders. Every new conquest of Hellenic civilization added an episode to his interminable legend. It is not always easy to decide whether certain of his wanderings, even to distant places, date from the time when these parts were first visited by Hellenes. For Heracles, I think, comes from the prehellenic 'Minoan' stratum of Greek civilization: and if, for example, he has certain adventures in Thrace, who is to decide whether these Thracian stories belong to the era of the Greek settlements in the Chersonese or to an earlier 'Minoan' occupation? But these doubts do not affect a great mass of details in the later legend of Heracles, which are clearly the results of travel and exploration in historical times.

Then there was the *Arimaspea*. The reputed author of this wild poem, the ancestor of as wild a progeny, was a certain Aristeas of Proconnêsus, an island in the Sea of Marmora. What we know of him comes from Herodotus.

'I will tell what I heard men say of him in Proconnêsus and Cyzicus. They say that Aristeas, who by birth was inferior to none of the citizens, went into a fuller's shop in Proconnêsus and there died. So the fuller locked the door of his shop, and went to tell the kinsmen of the dead man. But after the tidings had now been spread abroad in the town that Aristeas was dead, a man of Cyzicus, who had come from the city of Artaca, entered into debate with those who told the tale, saying that he had met Aristeas on the road to Cyzicus and had speech with him. Now as this man was earnestly disputing the matter, the kinsmen of the dead were come to the fuller's shop with that which was needful for the burial. But when the building was opened—no sign of Aristeas, dead or alive! But in the seventh year thereafter they say that he appeared in the flesh in Proconnêsus, and made those verses that are now called by the Greeks *Arimaspea* ; and when he had made them, vanished the second time.

'This then is what these cities say. But I will now tell of matters that befell among the Metapontines of Italy two hundred and forty years (as I discovered by comparing the stories) after the second disappearance of Aristeas. The Metapontines say that he showed himself bodily in their land, and bade them build an altar to Apollo, and set up thereby an image inscribed to *Aristeas of Proconnêsus*. "For Apollo visited their land only of the Greek cities in Italy, attended by him, Aristeas, whom they now saw before them ; but at the time when he went with the god, he was a raven". When he had spoken these words he vanished. And the Metapontines relate that they sent to Delphi and made question of the god, what the phantasm of the man portended. The prophetess bade them be obedient to the vision, if they hearkened to the vision it would be better for them in the end. They took this advice and performed the due rites. And so there now stands an image with the name of Aristeas beside the altar itself of Apollo, and round it stand laurel bushes; and the altar is set up in the market-place.

'I say no more then of Aristeas.'

In the poem which he left behind him Aristeas said that he had visited the tribes of the far north in obedience to a divine impulse. There was a story that he rode there on a golden arrow. Herodotus calls him *phoibolamptos*, a man inspired. He told of the Scythians and Issedonians, and of the Arimaspeans who are one-eyed men, and steal the treasure of the gold-guarding griffins. The story of the Arimaspeans and the griffins became very popular, so popular that the poem of Aristeas, who of course never thought of giving it a name himself any more than any other ancient poet, came to be called *Arimaspea*, 'The Arimaspean Verses'. The Arimaspeans and the griffins come into the *Prometheus Bound* of Aeschylus, who is as full as Marlowe or Hugo of echoing names borrowed from a romantic geography. They fascinated the Middle Ages. Sir John Mandeville 'had seen many a griffoun'. Aristeas did not go so far as that. 'Although he is writing poetry, he has not said that he went farther than the Issedonians.' The truth is that all this mythical matter may easily lead us to undervalue the merit of Aristeas as a geographer and ethnologist. He perceived, for instance, that the movements of the Scythians and Cimmerians in historical times were due to the Wanderings of the Peoples in Central Asia. And his geography appears to have been sound enough up to a point indicated by himself. We cannot doubt that his poem embodied the knowledge gathered by travellers and pioneers on the northern shore of the Black Sea.

About the end of the sixth century before Christ, Scylax of Caryanda, a Carian Greek, led an expedition for King Darius down some great 'crocodile'-haunted river, the Indus or the Ganges, and afterwards published an account of his voyage, which Herodotus doubtless read. The Persian Wars also drove a little geography into the most ignorant head. In particular the Greeks of the south awoke to the consciousness that they knew remarkably little about the lie of the land north of Thermopylae. There are traces of this ignorance surviving in Herodotus himself. But this is a trifling matter compared with the great conception of the *Orbis Herodoteus*. He lived in an age when it was possible to build up that.

He is himself a really great geographer; and his greatness and positive superiority to his predecessors consist chiefly in this, that he has no theory of what the form of the earth ought to be, but is content with it as it is. His attitude on the subject is agnostic and critical. So indeed is his whole intellectual temper—a fact not always adequately realized. He says more than once 'I am bound to repeat what is currently said'—observe that, it is the point of view of all early, spoken literature : the necessity of handing on the traditions—'but I am not in the least bound to believe it'. It is the second clause only that is really significant. In like manner the religion and morality of Herodotus are conventional; the apologetic scepticism, the demure irony are the man himself. For this reason he needs as wary reading as Heine. People talked about the Hyperboreans, men who lived beyond the north wind. 'But', Herodotus gravely argues, 'if there are *Hyperboreans* there must be *Hypernotians*, men who live beyond the south wind, too.' "An absurd argument", say his commentators. Why, yes. . . . But Herodotus was arguing with people who believed in a symmetrical earth.

But Herodotus' scepticism is not of the stupid, dogmatic sort. His Ulyssean life had taught him that '*anything* may be true', 'anything may happen in the course of time'. The popular impression of him is still, one gathers, that of a credulous, garrulous ancient, a little given to lying. The simple truth is that he will neither believe anything nor disbelieve anything without a reason which appears to himself at least plausible. Of course his canons of credibility are not ours; although they are not so very much less rigorous after all. The great thing is that he keeps an open mind. But he has a natural love of the marvellous, and he knows he can tell a story. So he tells it, and leaves the reader to make of it what he will. The reader, finding him full of prodigious tales, thinks that Herodotus must have been easily gulled. He was not easily gulled. It is possible that here and there he is gulling his readers. He has the genius of the historical novelist rather than the historian proper. There is more of Walter Scott in him than of Stubbs or Gardiner.

Besides, the instinct which prompted him not to

reject a story merely because it seemed improbable is a genuinely scientific one. That should be remembered to his credit. His method is being more and more justified every year. For it has given us stories which are not only exquisite pieces of narrative but are truer than his critics till the other day had dreamed. For instance, the story of certain young braves of the Nasamonians who got lost in the Sahara. They journeyed for days across the desert, until they came to an oasis. As they were plucking the fruit of the trees there, they were attacked by dwarfs who seized and carried them off. The dwarfs talked in an unknown tongue. They conveyed their prisoners over great marshes to a settlement of the pygmies, tiny black men like themselves. A great river, with crocodiles in it, flowed past their kraals. The natives (as the Nasamonians reported on their safe return) were 'all sorcerers'. The story is true. The river was the Niger, the native town—who knows?

One reason why Herodotus is so good upon geography is that he has the imagination of the explorer.

He is a wonderful observer. 'The Maxyes shave the left side of their heads and let the hair grow long on the right; and they colour their bodies vermilion.' You see the Maxyes? Writing like that makes us discontented with the indirectness of modern speech. But Herodotus does not mean to be pictorial, simply. He is picturesque because he happens to be a master of style, because he cannot help it, because he is 'a man for whom the visible world exists'. But he is also an anthropologist, interested in the habits of the Maxyes on account of their human significance. What kind of men are they who do such things? What makes them

do it ? The answer of the geographer Herodotus is :
Partly their physical environment. He does not put
it in that jargon, but characteristically in the form of a
story, the epilogue to his book.

'Artembares was the author of that counsel, which
the Persians accepted, and commended to Cyrus in
words like these : *Seeing that God hath given govern-
ance to the Persians and among men, O Cyrus, to thee ;
now that He hath put down Astyages, come, for our land
is narrow and barren, let us remove out of it and occupy
a better. There be many lands nigh to us, and many also
farther off, whereof if we get one we shall be held in far
greater honour. And meet is it that men that are rulers
should do such things. For when shall there be indeed a
fairer opportunity than now when at least we are rulers
over many men and the whole of Asia ?* But Cyrus,
hearing these words and misliking their purport, bade
the Persians do this thing if they would, but counselled
them to prepare in that event to be no longer rulers
but to be ruled of others. For of a soft land were
wont to be born soft men, seeing it was in no wise
given to the same land to bring forth delightful fruits
and good fighters. Therefore the Persians, assenting
to his words, withdrew themselves and departed,
being changed in their opinion by Cyrus, and chose
to dwell on an ungrateful soil and exercise rule rather
than to sow the valley and be the slaves of others.'

THUCYDIDES

ANCIENT writers when they speak of themselves are
usually content to relate their experiences; or if they
tell us of their emotions, they do not analyse them.
Their psychology is creative, not analytic; the
psychology of the dramatist, not of the philosopher
and the man of science. There is hardly any attempt
at the exact description of emotional states. When
such an attempt is made, it is nearly always curiously
naive, inadequate, and conventionally phrased. They
knew what people felt, they could wonderfully
dramatize the expression of their feelings in significant
actions; but they could not analyse them. They did
not think of them at all. Ancient egotism was not of
the introspective kind. It was too social for that, too
deeply absorbed in the game of life. It is the solitary
who examines his emotions—the outcast, the rebel, the
saint. Such characters were exceedingly rare in old
Greece; and if they spoke, they would scarcely have
found an audience; and if they wrote a book, it was
not likely to be made public. Where the state counts
for everything, the social emotions eat up the individual.
Now the ancient man was not merely in the community,
he was of it, you might almost say a mode of its
expression. A 'private citizen' was either disloyal or
an 'idiot'. The great men of antiquity were those who

shared the common thoughts and aspirations with the intelligence and intensity of genius. Anatole France makes a character in one of his novels say of Napoleon that he thought what every grenadier in his army thought, only with a greater force. Just as Napoleon was the child of the Revolution, every great Greek was the child of his Polis. Pericles is Athens in one of her moods, Cleon is Athens in another. That is why they appear to us so shadowy and impersonal, why they look more like types than individuals.

This impression is heightened for us by the manner in which it is conveyed. We view the men of antiquity almost solely through the medium of ancient art; and ancient art (by which I mean here more particularly Greek literature) is animated by a spirit which modern literature has upon the whole repudiated. Greek art is traditional and conventional; the modern spirit is private and impatient of tradition, and has made ' conventional ' a word of reproach. The contradiction is not so absolute in fact as it looks when stated in words. The Greek artist always brought something of his own to the conventional theme or *motif* which he was treating, while we, who in our morn of youth defy the conventions, visibly suffer when our own standards come to be challenged in their turn. In reality of course the artist can no more escape from all the conventions than he can afford to become a copier. But my immediate point is this. Greek art, permitting the utmost freedom of treatment within certain limits, insisted on the observance of these limits. Modern art rejects, at least in theory, any limitation at all, even (when the theory is carried to its logical issue) the limits of sanity. What the modern poet seeks above everything else is originality. The ancient poet avoided the appearance of originality. He treated a traditional theme in a conventional style and form, making it in fact the main part of his artistic effort that he should preserve the convention. But he does not merely reproduce, he renovates it. It issues from his imagination like Aeson from the cauldron which renewed his youth. Every detail receives the significance it has for the poet and for no other man before him. So Greek poetry, extraordinarily conservative in form, may become and is in fact truly original, the most original in the world. And what is true of Greek poetry is true of Greek literature in general, even of history, which the ancients regarded as an art and subject to the laws of artistic convention like any other art.

The historian indeed is not bound by the convention in the same way as the poet, for the reason that form, although not more essential, is much stricter and more clearly defined in poetry than in prose. The historian may choose a new subject and write of it in a new style. But that instinct for continuing the tradition as a thing in itself of infinite spiritual and artistic value moves the Greek in other ways. It affects his psychology, which is content to deal with certain traditional concepts that to our minds put it out of almost all relation to reality. Man is the puppet of Contention, Desire, Temptation, Hope, which are imagined as external forces, personified or half personified Daemons. This theory is nowhere crudely stated even in Herodotus, for it was not fully thought out. But it is implied in the psychology not only of Herodotus but of Thucydides also. It was the traditional theory, the popular belief; the historians merely qualify and refine it. It could never have satisfied so clear an intellect as Thucydides. But he uses it as far as he can, largely perhaps for want of a more precise terminology. Clearly, in a psychology of this sort, the qualities which compose what we call a ' personality ' will have little significance. A man becomes the embodiment of a single ' ruling passion ', good or evil. Aristides becomes the Just Man, Pericles the Magnanimous Man, Cleon the Violent Man. It is all much too simple, naive, and romantic, and it is slightly exasperating to an age which reads Dostoevsky and Henry James. It seems to take no account of mixed motives at all. One can see the effect of this even so late as Tacitus. He has a way—it is very unscrupulous if he knows better—of stating a dilemma of this form : ' Tiberius acted so either from this good motive or from that bad one.' And, partly because the good motive usually wears an aspect of extreme unplausibility, partly because ' we demen gladly to the bader end,' the character of Tiberius suffers. That the emperor may have acted on grounds, some of which were creditable to him and some not, is never suggested. Yet no ancient historian approaches Tacitus in the acuteness of his feeling for character.

We cannot complain that ancient writers are reticent. But it is always ' What I saw ' or ' What I think is the reason ' ; it is never ' How did this affect my outlook upon life ? ' ' What spiritual activities did it call into play ? ' Herodotus is constantly speaking in the first person ; it is usual to call him ' garrulous '. Does any one feel that he knows Herodotus, really ? Again, Socrates was constantly discussing himself, talking without reserve about his most intimate feelings. We know all about him; we should recognize him in the street. But are not scholars still disputing about the 'real' Socrates?

When people say of Thucydides that the man is an enigma because he is so reticent, they are stating the case in a misleading way. He is not more enigmatic than Herodotus or Xenophon, whose character, in spite of the *Anabasis*, is so featureless to us that we can make hardly anything of it. It is certainly true that Thucydides is reticent. No other prose writer of antiquity is so reserved, or reserved in just that way. But therefore, by a curious paradox, the very reticence of Thucydides helps us to understand him. It is a trait of character.

He was the son of Olorus, a Thracian name, and on that side his blood was noble, even princely. He was the cousin of Cimon, the leader of the oligarchic party in Athens. He inherited great wealth, drawn chiefly from gold mines on his estates in Thrace. He had the very greatest ability. . . . No fairer combination of opportunities could have been contrived for a young man who proposed, like Thucydides, to enter public life. He rose to high office in the service of the state, was put to the test, and—failed. For twenty years he lived in exile, only returning to Athens at the end of the war, which he did not long survive. He had meant to be a soldier and statesman. Instead, he wrote a book, full of practical wisdom, of high military sagacity, revealing a grasp of affairs and the trend of political forces which we do not find again till we come to Polybius. He could not have failed from incapacity; and he had all the chances. To what then was his failure due?   To an accident, to an error of judgement, to a flaw of character?

He does not tell us himself; and we have not the materials for an opinion.   While he was away with his fleet at Thasos, he let Brasidas surprise Amphipolis. That is all we know.   But although we cannot say why this should have happened, we can estimate the probable effect of the incident and of its consequences upon the mind of Thucydides.   For no history ever written, not even *The French Revolution*, is fuller of the *ethos* of its writer.   You cannot read the first five sentences of Thucydides without feeling that no one before or since has written quite like that.   We can study this idiosyncrasy of the author and the interrelations between it and the events of his life.   The impression one receives from this study is necessarily coloured by one's own temperament and general attitude to things.   But stating it is at any rate a legitimate form of criticism.

The youth of Thucydides was passed—it was another of his opportunities—in an age and a place where life was more vivid and intense and interesting than perhaps it has ever been since.   Athens was recovering from the disasters which had ended in the humiliating Thirty Years Peace (446–445 B.C.).   She was showing an incredible vitality.   Her Empire or Rule (as she too fondly called it), if less far flung, was better organized and more securely held than ever.   No state of Greece had achieved half so much, or possessed a power like hers.   And her energy strained her material resources to the utmost.   "They have the pioneering spirit", said the Corinthians about the people they hated so, "quick to form new plans, quick to put them into execution . . . ready to take risks, facing danger with a lifting of the heart. . . . They make the most of a success, they give way the least under defeat. An Athenian spends himself in the service of his city as if his body were not his own, and counts his mind then most his own when it is employed upon her business. When a plan of theirs breaks down, they think they have been cheated; when it succeeds, it is an instalment of triumphs to come. . . . Their whole life is a round of toils and dangers. Their passion for getting leaves them no time for enjoying. Their *one* idea of a holiday is doing their duty, and the most irksome task is better to them than a public sinecure. So that if one were to sum up the matter by saying that they were born neither to rest themselves nor to let other people rest, he would not be far wrong." And Pericles said: "Our enterprise has burst the bars of every sea and every land, and wherever we have settled has left imperishable monuments of the benefits and the injuries we bestow." There survives a stone with this inscription:

Of the Erechtheid Tribe,
There were slain in the war in Cyprus, in Egypt, in
Phoenice, at Halieis, in Aegina, at Megara, in the same year,
These . . .

and then the names. That was as early as 459 B.C.

Along with all this fighting and colonizing effort went a corresponding economic development. Ancient historians are almost silent about it; partly because they took for granted a general knowledge on their readers' part of economic conditions in Greece, partly because, being men of letters rather than statesmen or merchants, they did not realize the importance in history of the economic factor. It is possible to overestimate it.   There is to my way of thinking a tendency to overestimate it now, at any rate in its effects on ancient history.   The city-state was, by our standards, so extraordinarily self-denying and 'self-sufficing'— although Athens imported most of its food—that the problems which are perhaps the chief preoccupation of the modern statesman really did not concern it so vitally.   Thucydides, who makes so little of all these questions of trade routes and food supply, and gives so clear a prominence to the idealistic Funeral Speech of Pericles, gives us after all the right approach to Athenian history.   For herself as much as for us Athens was always a 'city of God'.   Even the Theban Pindar called her that.   No state more passionately embraced the doctrine that man cannot live by bread alone.   The Piraeus might think differently, and the tradesmen-politicians might fill the city with docks and arsenals.   But in her heart she knew that these things were, if not 'rubbish' as Plato said, at any rate the least part of her achievement.   The Athenians wanted them too, of course.   They wanted to make Athens queen of the world because—well, because she was so beautiful. This is not my language but Pericles'.   It is the language of artists and idealists.   It is only the modern departmental view of the artist's life that falls to the assault of the economist.   No Greek was content to be an artist with a single part of his brain.   He put the signature of his personality upon everything he did— even if it were, as the epitaph of Aeschylus boasts, the right cleaving of the skull of a long-haired Mede.   The instinct of the world is right ; the Greeks were essentially artists.   They were dreamers striving to make their dream come true, striving to remould the world nearer to the heart's desire. They were not tradesmen extending the business.

'To live well': that was the true end of the state. Athens made what must be accounted the most successful effort ever made by any community to live well. There were no poets, no artists like her own ; yet she drew to herself the artists and thinkers of all Greece. It was the age of Phidias and the building of the Parthenon, of Sophocles, of Ionian science and the Sophists. No aspect of the genius of Athens was unfelt by Thucydides. The Speech of Pericles proves that. The patriotism of which it is the expression is the devotion of the thinker and the artist as much as of the soldier and the statesman. And all these devotions are fused in one passion, a passion like that of a lover for his mistress. Pericles sees his Athenians 'gazing upon Her and becoming her lovers'; and this seems to be one of his authentic utterances. For Athens is 'an education' for the rest of the world, and her citizens 'care for Beauty and Wisdom without weakness or extravagance'. These famous sentences, unforgettable in the Greek, curiously disappointing in translation, breathe the temper of the age. It is the spirit of Euripides' early dramas with their passionate romantic patriotism. It is the spirit of the great ode in the *Antigone* (442–441 B.C.) celebrating the Progress of Man, with its opening so natural to an Athenian :

> *Of many a marvellous thing*
> *Marvel of marvels is Man,*
> *Who for his wayfaring*
> *Hath-taken the whole sea's span;*
> *When the deep is a glimmer of foam*
> *In the wake of the storm-wind's wrath,*
> *Where the great seas heave and comb*
> *He cleaveth a path.*

And year by year man tilleth the Earth, though she is the eldest of the gods. And he captures and tames the wild birds of the air, and the wild creatures of wood and hill, and the brood of the sea. And he has found speech and thought, and the instinct to live in cities— how Greek all this is!—and his devices are without end. Only from Death there is no escape. Yet hath Man found remedies for many diseases.

To the Funeral Speech Thucydides gave a world of labour and thought. In style it is the most characteristic part of the History ; and it is also, as we might almost infer from that, the most characteristic in spirit. It is a statement of the Periclean ideal as Thucydides conceived it. How much of Pericles himself is in it we can hardly say now ; there is certainly a great deal of Thucydides. He has woven into it many memories of many speeches of the great statesman, and interpreted all for himself and his readers in these laboured, artificial sentences, which seem purposely to veil their meaning. The eloquence of the Funeral Speech is more in the thought than in the words of it. But the eloquence is so great as to make even Demosthenes appear a little empty and rhetorical by comparison. The emotion is so restrained, that a superficial reader will scarcely notice it, and will feel that Thucydides is 'cold'. Even good scholars have called him 'unemotional'. I cannot say how much I dissent from this judgement. 'Undemonstrative' if you like, but not unemotional. My whole assent goes with those whose interpretation of Thucydides' mind begins with the conviction that he shared to the full that passion of love and service to Athens, and that his book is the record of a shattered dream.

Such a view contradicts all our first impressions : so much is admitted. Thucydides appears the very embodiment of dispassionate reason. His standards are all intellectual. With him Virtue, it has been remarked, is apt to mean Brains ; and he has been compared to Machiavelli. He is contemptuous of the myths, which formed what might be called the romantic material of Greek literature. I had almost called them the only material ; certainly a Greek audience did not readily listen to anything else. 'You will not find Romance in my book', he says in effect ; 'you must go to Herodotus for that!' To Herodotus or the Logographers, the compilers of local legends. He is unsentimental, even for a Greek. He has no Moral Tales like the Fable of Solon in Herodotus. There are times when the reader is almost angry with him for not expressing his disapproval of some monstrous cruelty or injustice. It looks cynical to say nothing ; yet Thucydides says nothing.

This clearly requires explanation ; and I think any explanation would seem unsatisfactory which did not allow for an original bias or quality in Thucydides. No sensitive criticism can fail to detect in him a certain arrogance or pride of intellect. It is part of the pride I take to be characteristic of the man ; or rather it is the form in which that pride most naturally expresses itself. He says things like these. 'My book is not written for immediate popularity, but to possess a lasting value.' Nicias did not merit his dreadful end, for 'he lived in the performance of everything that is accounted virtue'. That is not perhaps a sneer, but it is a reservation. Thucydides implies that he would not himself judge Nicias by that standard, but by another, more intellectual one ; measured by which, Nicias was—well, a failure. Observe how he is attracted by proud, intellectual, 'superior' men : Pericles, Antiphon. He says about Homer ' if any one thinks his evidence good enough '. He says of Brasidas that he was a good speaker ' for a Lacedaemonian '. His attitude to his predecessors in historical writing is not merely critical, like the attitude of Polybius, but slightly supercilious. He scarcely deigns to mention them. No doubt he often sets Hellanicus right without comment. He clearly believed that he himself was the first to write history as it ought to be written.

But this propensity was undoubtedly confirmed in him by certain tendencies of the day. Thucydides appears to have felt them with that seemingly incompatible mixture of impressionability and detachment which is characteristic of the Greek genius, and perhaps of all artistic genius. They may be summarized by describing his age as the Greek Age of Reason. Nothing was to be accepted as true which did not commend itself to the reason. No more superstition, no more myths, no more false sentiment, no more cant or conventionality ; let us get at once to the Truth of Things ! Alas for the twentieth century, we have heard that cry so often now ! It has not lost its power to inspire ; but somehow Truth does not seem any nearer. In those days it seemed very near ; thanks to Reason or Intelligence. At first 'all things were mixed up', said Anaxagoras ; then *Nous* came and 'arranged' them. The sun was not a god ; it was a white-hot mass ' bigger than the Peloponnese ', and the moon had houses in it, and hills, and ravines. Protagoras said ' Respecting the gods I cannot say that they exist, nor yet that they do not exist. For there are many things which prevent this knowledge: the darkness of the subject, and the shortness of human life'. Gorgias used reason to confute the senses. Our knowledge comes from the senses; the senses are untrustworthy witnesses; and so there is no such thing as certainty. He held that, first, *Nothing exists*; secondly, *if it did exist, we could not know it*; thirdly, *if we could know it, we could not communicate our knowledge*. This is the very *hubris* of intellectualism. The Sophists, it appears, were in the habit of contrasting things which existed by 'nature' with things which existed by 'law' or custom or conventionality—*Nomos*. Herodotus, who is not to be called a Sophist, but was not unaffected by the tendencies which produced the Sophistic movement, has a story to illustrate this antithesis. When Darius was king, he asked some Greeks whom he had summoned to his presence how much they would take to eat their dead fathers. They replied that they would not do it for anything! Darius then sent for the Indian people called the Callatiae, who eat their parents, and asked them before the Greeks, who had use of an interpreter, for how much money they would be prepared to burn the bodies of their fathers with fire. The Indians shouted loudly and bade him hold his peace. Herodotus adds: 'I think Pindar is right when he says *Custom is Lord of All*'. So then, the Sophists were tempted to ask, may not Justice, Morality, Religion itself be simply Custom, Convention? . . .

The philosophical value of Sophistic thought is perhaps not very great. It is rather childishly paradoxical, and it is grounded upon a very small induction

of facts. It set up a number of unreal antitheses—like
that one of Nature and Custom—of which philosophy
was long in ridding itself. But it was not truly sub-
versive either of patriotism or morality. To proclaim
the relativity of knowledge, as Protagoras did in his
famous 'sentence' *Man is the measure of all things* did
not in his case have any antisocial or nihilistic intention.
He was not thinking of Man but of men, individual
citizens of a city ; and so his doctrine did not come into
conflict at all with the claims of the state. Even to say
that religion and morality are conventions is not
necessarily to attack their validity or their claim upon
us for their observance. But in truth the Sophists did
not greatly concern themselves with questions of principle. They 'drove at practice'. They were apt to be
agnostic, to doubt if certainty be attainable. But they
meant to use their brains upon every subject that men
discussed. Admitting knowledge to be relative, they
meant to know everything. Man's chief end was to
know ; virtue was knowledge and vice a kind of
ignorance. Moreover knowledge, although it must give
up the pretence of being absolute, acquired by that very
surrender a new *practical* value. It fitted a man to
succeed in life. It became an instrument of social
service. Protagoras professed to teach 'Civic Virtue'.

But Civic Virtue, the quality which made a man
successful in public life, was hardly possible in the
ancient state without the art of speech. So Rhetoric,
defined as the Art of Persuasion, became all-important.
It was what the Sophists chiefly undertook to teach.
Thucydides heard Gorgias of Leontini address the
Athenian Assembly in favour of his native city, and
caught from him certain artifices of style which bewray

themselves especially in those passages of the History on which the author has spent most pains. These artifices have a curious effect on the reader. They seem somehow incompatible with perfect intellectual honesty; and yet Thucydides is manifestly, is passionately sincere. He must genuinely have admired the mechanical balance and antithesis, the unusual 'poetic' diction of Gorgias. He uses similar effects himself with great power, and is incapable of that triviality and tawdriness which would otherwise seem inseparable from the style. We must believe that the style itself, though 'obscure and contorted' as Dionysius complained, appeared to Thucydides to have wonderful new possibilities, some of which he did actually reveal. He had been searching for a style to fit the new 'modern' history he intended to write, and here was one ready to his hand. It suited him further because his thought was naturally antithetic, like the thought of all men with the gift of impartiality. But there was a deeper reason than either of these. The difficult style of Thucydides is the man himself. It is possible to divide authors into those whose originality consists in saying plainly what has never been said before, or never so plainly—'what oft was thought, but ne'er as well express'd';—and those whose originality is in the very structure of their minds, and makes a certain language natural in them, which would seem unnatural in any one else. Macaulay belongs to the first division, Carlyle to the second. Herodotus belongs to the first, Thucydides to the second. It is somewhat beside the point to argue that the style of Thucydides is comparatively plain and simple in the less laboured parts of his book. An artist must be judged by the finished products of his art, because it is in them that he most truly 'finds himself'. And after all, would the Speech of Pericles be equally moving in any other manner? That is the question to ask, if we wish to know whether Thucydides was a master of style.

The Peloponnesian War gave him his subject. He was sure that it was to be the greatest war that ever happened, and he was sure that he was the man to write its history. He intended to make his book a model of accuracy. He would set down everything just as it occurred, without extenuation or malice, accepting nothing merely because it had authority or tradition on its side. I think he agreed with Pericles that Athens would be victorious in the war, and believed that the simple truth would do her more honour than any array of words and arguments. She did not need Homer or any other singer of legendary glories to celebrate her power and beauty. These were manifest now and here. There had never been any city like her; that could be proved by scientific criticism. Homer's glorification of Mycenae was plainly Contrary to Reason. The war would end in the triumph of Athens and her ideals, and his book would be the faithful record of that triumph. . . .

The war began well for Athens. The prediction of Pericles was justifying itself. And then—'the Plague first began to occur among the Athenians'. The one contingency had happened against which no human wisdom could have provided. 'Never was such a pest or dying of men remembered.' The physicians, ignorant of the proper treatment of the malady, 'died themselves'. 'And supplications at temples or oracles, and all expedients of that kind—all were of no avail.

And in the end people gave them up, overmastered by the plague.' 'They lay one on top of the other in the article of death, or stumbled about the streets and wells, half-dead with thirst.' 'Many neglected patients threw themselves into the wells, being possessed by an unquenchable desire; drink as they liked, it made no difference. And they were tormented by a perpetual restlessness and insomnia.' 'The birds and beasts that feed on human flesh, in that glut of unburied carcasses yet fought shy of them, or if they touched them, died.'

The description of the Plague was one of the most celebrated things in ancient literature. It is intensely characteristic of Thucydides. It is exact and minute as an official report; it rigidly excludes any supernatural explanation; it is carefully unsensational. Withal it is unforgettably vivid, painful and pathetic. Thucydides has here given us an almost perfect example of his peculiar realism; and in many other places, as in the harrowing last scenes of the Sicilian campaign, his art is distinctly realistic. To relate, without suppression or distortion but with the vividness of the artist, every relevant thing that happened precisely as it happened—that is his aim in these passages, and that is realism. It goes naturally with the intellectual temper which insists on getting at 'the truth of things'; that temper which we find in Socrates and Euripides as well as in their contemporary Thucydides. It is, I think, exceedingly important to observe that this passion for the truth brings in an emotional element. The true realism is never coldly objective; the great Realists, we cannot but remember, have all been men of fiery convictions. Under words superficially unemotional is hidden a profound emotion. We feel it, although we cannot say exactly how it is communicated. Its communication is one of the secrets of genius, and this secret Thucydides possesses.

We might in any case infer that the memory of the Plague was branded upon his soul, for he was one of the few who were attacked by it and survived. No man could pass through such an experience and be the same afterwards. Thucydides tells us what he had to face. 'The worst of it was the despondency that seized a man whenever he felt himself growing ill; that, and the way people caught the infection while nursing one another and died like sheep. It was this that caused the highest mortality. For when people were afraid to visit one another, the sick died without attendance, and many households were blotted out of existence for want of some one to wait on their needs; and on the other hand, when they did visit, the visitors lost their own lives; and these were chiefly such as would be thought virtuous. For they went to the houses of their friends, nobly regardless of their personal safety; because at last the very relations of the dead ceased their wailing out of sheer exhaustion, overwhelmed by the extent of the disaster.' Those who recovered 'were congratulated by all the others, while they themselves in that moment of rapture cherished somehow a childish expectation that they would never die of any disease ever after'. Thucydides remembered that!

Here are some more of his memories. 'The sacred buildings, where some took up their quarters, were filled with dead, men dying actually *in* them'—an unspeakable horror this to Greek religious sentiment— 'the malady so tyrannizing over their minds that, not knowing what was to become of them, they disregarded sacred and profane alike. All the burial customs formerly in use were confounded, and the dead were disposed of to the best of every man's ability.' 'Also the Plague started a general increase of crime. Men ventured more boldy upon actions which they formerly professed to take no pleasure in. For now they saw how short was the swing between happiness and sudden death, between poverty and the unexpected inheritance of wealth. So they made haste to enjoy themselves, looking on their persons and their purses as given them to spend in a day. And nobody was anxious to labour in the cause of Honour; might he not die before he attained it?' 'Neither the fear of God nor the law of man was any restraint. Seeing all perish without distinction, men concluded that it made no difference whether you worshipped the gods or not. As for human offences, everyone expected that he would not live to pay the penalty for them. Far greater was the doom already pronounced on themselves and poised to fall. Before it fell, surely they might have one little taste of the sweetness of life?'

It is possible that the Plague left Thucydides a different man physically. His is not an enjoying nature; a little atrabilious perhaps. An illness which does not kill life will often kill the joy of it. One thinks of Carlyle, who is so like Thucydides in the combination of idealism with something like its opposite. Thucydides would have thought that Frederick the Great had 'virtue'. Of course a resemblance of that kind is not merely the result of physical causes. The spiritual effects of the Plague upon Thucydides can be more reasonably conjectured. For one who loved Athens with that intimate feeling which makes ancient patriotism seem so much more personal than ours, and was I think the passion of Thucydides' life, the mere disappointment must have been terrible. He had seen every restraint of religion, of morality, of ordinary decency even, give way under the stress of pain and fear and horror; and the people dying 'like sheep'; and no one knowing what the end would be. The History is always insisting on the mutability of human affairs. Athens would have won in the War, if the advice of Pericles had been followed; but Pericles died. The Sicilian Expedition would have succeeded but for a series of miscalculations started by a perfectly incalculable incident, the Mutilation of the Hermae. His military experience may have first taught him this distrust of fortune, but it must have been greatly deepened by the Plague. He had also seen how thin is the partition, not only between prosperity and ruin, but between virtue and vice; and that is a horrible experience. It made him, not exactly cynical, but terribly convinced of the weakness of human nature. The Plague was his first great disillusionment.

It did not pass away. The Plague left a new Athens infected with a spirit he could not share. Pericles fell into disfavour, and (though he quickly recovered his authority) died soon after, with what fears for his country we can imagine. The advocate of the new spirit was Cleon. He was one of those public men— Gifford and Croker are examples in English politics— who have a faculty of arousing an almost frantic hatred in men of genius. There was something about the very appearance of this man, his tones and gestures, which irritated educated and fastidious people like Thucydides and Aristophanes. They were annoyed by his raucous voice, his 'violence'. They thought him forward, ignorant, amazingly conceited; in a word, vulgar. It is quite probable that Cleon was all of these things. But he was also able, sincere, eloquent in a way, fearless, incorruptible; above all, he understood the point of view of the *bourgeoisie* to which he belonged, as the aristocrat Pericles could not. It ought to be remembered that all our information about Cleon comes from his political opponents, who may have shared Pericles' disability. For Cleon had made himself the mouthpiece of a new class in the state hitherto inarticulate, produced by the gradual democratization of Athens. This class had certainly some unlovely characteristics peculiarly distasteful to Thucydides. It was chauvinistic and philistine, and irreverent towards the Intellectuals; and it was bent on obtaining a living wage for every citizen, while Thucydides was wealthy and did not need to care about money. Even its patriotism probably struck him as unimaginative. He must have disliked Cleon before there was any question of his banishment. Very likely he came into conflict with him in the Ecclesia, for Thucydides would scarcely have been elected general unless he had come forward somewhat prominently in public discussions of military policy. He regarded Cleon as an amateur, at least in strategy. Cleon's theory that Sphacteria could be captured in a week or two was sheer madness. What matter although Sphacteria *was* captured within the time? It would not have happened but for a combination of most improbable accidents. He behaved like a fool at Amphipolis. All 'cool-headed' people would have been glad to get rid of him. . . .

Does the historian here abandon his habitual fairness? The question is often asked. I doubt if it can be answered by a simple yes or no. I think that to some extent he is unfair. But I cannot believe that he is moved by personal malice. Thucydides was too great and, let us add, too proud a man to let a motive of that kind influence his judgement. In some ways he is more than fair to Cleon. He puts into his mouth a speech of great force, acumen, and political courage. The stamp of Thucydides' literary genius is on that speech as it is on all the speeches, and Cleon never uttered it just so effectively as that. The historian in fact is following his regular practice of crystallizing in a single speech the spirit of a policy. Here it is the spirit of the party whereof Cleon was the spokesman, the party of 'violence'. Cleon becomes the representative of something far more elemental and significant than himself, becomes a type, 'the most violent of the citizens'. Thucydides is not moved so much by dislike of Cleon—although clearly he was vexed by his manners—as by dislike of the spirit he embodied. For that was hostile to the Periclean spirit. Cleon sneers at 'intellectual' people, hints that they were disloyal. The Athenians in his opinion were much too fond of art and literature and eloquence— 'like Sophists', he adds. They were too sentimental and quixotic, 'wanting some other than the hard facts of life'. A democracy of that kind, he scolded, could never manage an empire. Let us take a closer grip of the Allies, and cow them with an example of 'frightfulness'.—How all that would jar upon Thucydides with the great phrases of the Funeral Speech forever echoing in his memory, we can easily understand ; and understand, and almost forgive, when he calls a meaner successor of Cleon bluntly 'a rascal'.

Thucydides' opportunity came in 424, when as Stratêgos he sailed with a squadron of ships to match himself in Thrace against the brilliant Brasidas. He tells us the story of his failure with such meagreness of detail that it is impossible now to determine the rights and wrongs of his case. Rightly or wrongly, he was condemned to banishment, and remained in exile till the end of the war. It was a fortunate thing that, for Athens and for us, because it gave him special opportunities for acquiring information, and in particular because it allowed him an insight into the minds of the enemies of Athens and perhaps of some neutrals. It is a curious and teaching thing that Greek History is to a preponderant extent the work of men who were exiles or virtual exiles: Herodotus, Thucydides, Xenophon, Timaeus, Polybius. We cannot regret the circumstances which made Thucydides' book possible. But that he himself regretted them beyond measure, we cannot doubt. The History after all was but a second best, the best he could give *now*. We who habitually think of him as a man of letters have to force our imaginations a little to realize the measure of his disappointment. But it changed the world for Thucydides.

His own reticence about it is one of the most interesting things in literature. Such a silence was far more difficult for an ancient than for a modern writer. An author of to-day can afford to ignore a personal attack in the confidence that sooner or later the true facts of the case will come to light. Thucydides had no such consolation. There were no reliable sources of information, no Blue Books accessible to the public. Books of any kind were extremely rare and costly, and consequently little read.   In public discussion, of which there was more than enough, the merits of a case were sure to be obscured or distorted.   As a result ancient literature is full of apologias, and self-justifications, and personal attacks on political opponents.   These things displease us, for we suspect the man who is always loudly proclaiming the purity of his motives.   One sometimes wishes about Demosthenes himself that he would refrain from so much public washing of linen. We have to stimulate ourselves to remember that a Greek statesman could scarcely help himself.   To let your case go by default was in Greek eyes an admission of guilt.   To treat a public accusation against you with silent contempt seemed to the average Athenian not only absurd but, I fear, merely unintelligible.   Pericles might do it.   But then everybody knew that the charges against him were lies.   They were just jokes of the Comic poets and that scandalous Stesimbrotus, who wasn't an Athenian at all.   The position of Thucydides was quite different.   He had been condemned on a grave charge of incompetence or treachery or cowardice. And the man will not defend himself!   He fills his book with the apologies of unscrupulous politicians, lets everybody have a fair hearing but himself.   Did he really feel that his case was indefensible?   Were there *no* extenuating circumstances?   That is so unpleasant for us to believe, that historians have tried to find them for Thucydides.   He will not find them for himself.   What a pride, or what a confession!

But there is a passage in which he describes the kind of man who failed in the war, and the reasons for his failure. However impartially Thucydides might try to discuss that question, he could not have prevented his own experience from influencing his judgement. His view then is that it was the non-party man who failed. Now Thucydides is himself a non-party man. The best constitution Athens ever had, he thought, was formed by a due admixture of oligarchic and democratic elements. The war brought no greater evil in its train than the exacerbation everywhere of the party spirit. 'The leading politicians on both sides, while ostensibly promoting what they eloquently called "the equality of all classes in the state before the law", or (on the other side) "sensible government by the Best", merely turned to their own uses the public interests they pretended to conserve, and in the heat of their personal rivalries ventured on the most atrocious actions, pursuing their revenges to the utmost, both sides disregarding every consideration of justice or public expediency, and defining their obligations by what suited them at the time, and all alike prepared to satiate the spirit of faction by contriving an unjust verdict against an opponent or securing the mastery by force.' 'Words no longer bore the same relations to things, but had their meaning wrested to suit the speaker's mind. Inconsiderate daring was "the courage that makes a good comrade", prudent delay "a fine name for cowardice", cool reflection "the caitiff's excuse", to know everything was "to do nothing". Frenzied activity was "the true part of a *man*", to think out a safe plan of attack was "a specious excuse for shirking". The extreme man was always trusted, his opponent suspect.' 'For the most part it was the stupider sort who saved themselves. For conscious of their own deficiency and the superior intelligence of their enemies, and fearing that they would get the worst of it in public debate, and that the subtle wits of their opponents would devise a scheme against them before they were ready, they acted at once ; while their victims, presuming in their arrogance that they would spy the first sign of an attack, and that there was no necessity actively to secure what they would get by the use of their brains, were apt to be caught off their guard, and met their end.'

Surely these are significant sentences, coming from such a man. "In the Greece of my time", we may imagine Thucydides saying, "there was no room for the man who would not sell his soul to a faction, who had too much intellectual honesty to make a shibboleth of a party cry, who hated the general debasement of the moral currency, who wanted to reflect before he acted." The popular answer to that indictment was: 'the man who will not act till he knows everything will never act at all' (τὸ πρὸς ἅπαν ξυνετὸν ἐπὶ πᾶν ἀργόν). It makes us think of Hamlet, who was no mere dreamer either, but had 'the courtier's, soldier's, scholar's, eye, tongue, sword.' Thucydides may well have been overintellectual for a successful man of action. His mind is naturally subtle. Observe that curious touch about the clever and the stupid man, how the clever man paid the penalty for his contempt of the other's brains. And then consider this striking sentence : 'Simplicity, the principal element in lofty character, was laughed away'. Simplicity —'silly simplicity' in the original meaning of the word —could anything seem less characteristic of Thucydides himself? It was not characteristic of the Athenians, who, Herodotus tells us, were 'the farthest removed in my time from silly simplicity '.   But Thucydides means that honesty of purpose which thinks no evil and is easily imposed upon, the quality which reaches a kind of sublimity in Dostoevsky's Idiot. Why does Thucydides, generally so impatient of anything like stupidity, seem to praise it here ?   Because he feels that after all it is a finer thing to be an honest simple-minded man than to use your brains merely to get the better of your neighbour.   A politician should not be a fool, he thinks ; but —what a life our politicians lead !

There is another character in whom Thucydides could not but feel a peculiar interest, I mean of course the exile.   It must be this interest, I think, which as much as anything else accounts for the long digressions in the First Book upon the last days of Pausanias and Themistocles ; for in principle Thucydides objects to digressions.   These were in their time the two most famous men in Greece.   They were powerful, able, arrogant men, and in the end both fell upon evil days and were cast off by the states they had served so well. The same fate befell the brilliant Alcibiades.   The psychology of the Greek exile is difficult for us to understand.   It seems a strange and rather horrible thing that a patriot should suddenly become a traitor. Greek history is full of these traitors, exiles scheming revenge, dreaming day and night of red retribution upon the city which gave them birth.   Such were Pausanias and Themistocles and Alcibiades.   The explanation of their behaviour lies in the character of ancient patriotism, which Pericles, we remember, described as a form of love.   The exile felt towards his country as the discarded lover may feel towards his mistress, when he will do anything, commit any crime, to find relief for his heart.   So the Greek exile was prepared to betray his city to her enemies, in order that amid her ruins he might gloat over his ' return '—*euersa felix moriturus in urbe.*   Clearly such a man was half mad.   But think what his city must have meant to him in the days when he was still permitted to serve her.   Is modern patriotism as intense?

Thucydides had loved Athens like that.   But he at least could find no satisfaction in contriving her ruin. The wound he felt could not be healed with blood ; that way, he knew as well as Euripides, lay misery and madness.   Thucydides was too sane and too proud and too noble to feel like Alcibiades or those Corcyrean exiles, whose frenzy moves him to an implied rebuke. So far as we know, he did not even intrigue for his restoration.   The impartiality of his book is a proof not merely of his high conscience as a historian, but of an extraordinary magnanimity.   Think of the way in which Dante rages against Florence.   There was much in common between the men.   Both were proud, sensitive, austere, conscious of the possession of genius. Both had risen high in the public service, and both had suffered banishment.   But Thucydides does not rage against Athens.   Perhaps it was just this gift of dispassionate judgement which prevented him from being a poet. But it certainly lends him a wonderful moral dignity.

He knew of a different and finer revenge.   He would not rage or complain or defend himself; but he would tell the truth about Athens ; nothing more, but also nothing less.   He would tell the story of her gradual degeneration from the Athens of his youth, how she had alienated the noblest of her sons and given herself to her Cleons and Hyperboluses ; till the day of her humiliation came, when the Lacedaemonians took the Long Walls. Then he would be able to say to the world and to posterity "Judge between her and me".

And after all he could not do it. He has done his best. He has had no pity for Athens, no demonstrable pity. He has shown her 'the tyrant city', cruel, calculating, cynical, violent, overweening.—It is not true that Athens was habitually cruel; she was famous for her 'philanthropy'. But Thucydides will not leave her with a rag of self-respect; he shows that when it suited her she could be cruel enough.—She was not habitually cynical; you cannot have great art in an atmosphere of cynicism. But Athenian statesmen in Thucydides speak like Prussian officials. "What right", we can hear him saying, "what right has Athens to boast of her 'ideals' if she chooses leaders like these?" She had been false (we understand) to *his* ideals; that is what Thucydides cannot forgive in her. And what had she got by the betrayal? If she had followed the counsels of Pericles, there would have been no Sicilian disaster, no final surrender. She had only herself to blame. Thucydides might have used the very words of Dante to Florence: *S' io dico 'l ver, l'effetto nol nasconde*—'if I speak the truth, the facts do not hide it'. And so all the facts are set down, relentlessly.

And yet somehow the hard words do not deceive us. Read, for instance, the account of the final defeat in the Harbour of Syracuse and the disastrous retreat which followed. Even to us, two thousand years from the event, the pity of it is sharp. Was there no pity in the heart of the writer?—We are almost glad that the History was left unfinished, that he had not to describe the moment when the wail went up from Peiraeus to the City, and the pride of his Mistress was humbled at last.

GREEK COUNTRY LIFE

IT is one of the hardest things to realize that the old Greek civilization was more characteristically urban than our own. This difficulty is the result chiefly perhaps of two impressions. The modern imagination, oppressed by the stained skies and disturbing problems of our prodigious cities, is particularly struck by everything in Greek life which is most in contrast with all that—the pure light and delicate air, the little towns by the seashore or mountain-built with peaceful citadel, everything open to the fields and hills. In the second place the Greek temperament gives us the impression of being more spontaneous and unembarrassed in its expression than the English, with the result that we tend to think of the Greek as living in closer communion with nature, because he is nearer the 'natural man'. These impressions are not in themselves misleading. But they mislead us if we think in terms of the modern state.

We live and act politically by nations and empires. The ancient Greek belonged to the *Polis*. The word which meant 'city' meant also 'state'. Greek history is a record of the relations between a number of self-governing cities, sovereign and free. Except in a few isolated districts, where primitive conditions maintained themselves for a time, the countryman counted himself

5

a 'citizen'. His whole political status was defined by his relation to the city, although he might rarely visit the place except to vote. All questions of public policy were decided there. And, as we know, the old Greek life blossomed in the cities, not in the fields. It is of course true that civilization has always tended to concentrate itself in towns. But no people has ever taken the stamp of civic institutions like the Greek. Greek literature gives the point of view of the Milesian, the Athenian, the Alexandrian citizen. Rarely in the great days does it give us the national, 'panhellenic' standpoint. The point of view of the rustic it scarcely gives at all. We do find it in Hesiod almost unqualified in spite of an artificial diction. But Aristophanes idealizes, Theocritus idealizes.

Yet it is essential to our understanding of Greek literature, and even of Greek art and philosophy, to know what the country-dweller thought and felt. It is essential for the very reason that he was so inarticulate. We are apt to forget him. But he is there all the time, an immense silent influence. The absolute supremacy of the Polis in all the higher activities of life was paid for with a price. Life in the country became canalized. Sometimes it threatened to become stagnant. That was whenever the cities slackened a little in their heroic, pathetic struggle towards *ta kala*, the Beautiful Things. Then of course, when all has been said, ancient life was fundamentally agricultural and pastoral. The city could not sever itself from the countryside which fed it. Even Athens or Corinth or Rhodes, for all the ships in their harbours, had largely the character of a country town as compared with London, let us say, or New York. Every Greek city recognizably expressed the distinctive character of its hinterland. And just as it had sprung like Erechtheus from the soil, so the city constantly tended to sink back into it; I mean, morally and intellectually. This need not have been always an undesirable result. At least that is not my point. But I do think it very important to observe that throughout Greek history the countryman represents the unchanging and fundamental element. His thought is the permanent basis of all Hellenic thought.

Greece is geographically the southward slope of the Balkan highlands gradually sinking till they are quite submerged, all but the summits we call the Aegean Islands. The mountains are very high. Even in the south of the Peloponnese the wall of Taygetus towers nearly eight thousand feet over Sparta, steep as the side of a battleship. Thus within a few miles of each other you have Alpine and subtropical conditions. From palm and orange the eye rises to vine and olive, from olive to the evergreen oak, from oak to pine and heath. These different levels breed distinct types of men. The growers of figs and vines and olives differ widely from, and naturally dislike, the shepherd and the goatherd. For the goats *will* descend to nibble the young vineshoots when the boy is asleep in the sun. And the dog at the lowland farm comes back at dawn from the hill with specks of blood and wool about his jaws. So quarrels arise, the standing quarrels between the plains and the heights. Ancient literature tells us most about the plains. Very rarely we catch sight of some uncouth mountaineer, his body wrapped in the skin of a bear or a goat, wild-haired, grasping his curious stick. We can only guess at his thoughts.

Dimly we can guess at them. They have left their impress upon Greek religion. Certain myths and divinities and rituals are manifestly the product, and reflect the ways, of a pastoral society. Goat-footed Pan piping in some ravine lit up by the red-flowering oleander, or under a rock overbrowed by a stunted wild figtree, or in the broader shadow of mast-dropping oaks, is clearly an imagination of the goatherds. Some of the loveliest fancies of mythology—Pan catching the Moon in his misty fleeces; the Hind with the Golden Horns passing inviolate through the midnight forests—have come to us from the mountains of Arcadia. What did these stories mean to the men who told them first? Something more, although doubtless something less also, than they mean to us. They come to us enriched with all the associations of the poetry since written about them. Therefore they touch our imaginations. But not our practice or our beliefs. The Greek shepherd on the other hand believed the stories and acted upon his faith. We all admit that. It is indeed so much taken for granted that we do not try to think out all that is implied in the admission. It is just this imaginative laziness which has brought reproach upon classical studies. "Why trouble about origins?", a certain type of scholar cries, "what we want is the finished product." And so, because he does not know from what wild roots of life the masterpiece has grown, he talks about it in that unreal, external way which puts the unacademic man in a rage. . . .

Consider the life of shepherds in sparsely inhabited mountainous countries. These men at certain times of the year will be alone on the hills for days and nights together. They are so lonely that their speech becomes hoarse and indistinct. They avoid a stranger with an almost animal shyness, or else greet him with a pathetic eagerness. Often they go mad. Great parts of Greece were, and are, wilder than the wildest parts of Argyleshire or Connemara. In Arcadia they wore pig-skins and lived on acorns like the pigs. They hunted bears and wolves in the glens with javelins. They had savage dogs which they kept in order by throwing stones at them, and which would sometimes venture to attack and devour an unwary traveller. The men themselves were nearly as savage as their dogs. They lived in a kind of dumb communion with their flocks which is not only unintelligible but almost unimaginable to the civilized man. The characteristic Arcadian god was a goat, or rather half a goat. (The other half was shaped like a man. Just think what dim incredible fancies went to the forming of that divine monster!). Of course even Arcadian shepherds gradually shook themselves clear of mere barbarism. But they never got so far away from it as we are apt to suppose. In Plato's time they offered a human sacrifice to the god of Mount Lycaeus. If a man tasted of the single human entrail mingled with the other entrails of the victim, they believed that he was changed into a wolf. If the werewolf abstained so long from human flesh, in the ninth year he recovered human form ; but if he did not abstain, he remained a wolf still. They knew people to whom this had happened. The Arcadians were the oldest race under the moon. Nay, they were older than the moon herself. A king of Arcadia was the first man. They could let you see the cave where God was born, and point out the mountain top where he was buried. It is clear from such stories, and from all that we can learn about the conditions of their life, that these Peloponnesian shepherds were unspeakably poor and ignorant. Many of them could never have seen a Polis in all their days. At best they knew the villages down in the valley, which they visited now and then with their fleeces and goat's milk cheese. They were so ignorant of the sea that they might mistake an oar for a winnowing-fan. Now and again one of them, more enterprising than the others, would go and enlist in a body of mercenaries, and see fighting in Thrace or Asia. The rest remained behind, above the stream of human progress.

The lowland farmer had a much more sociable and normally comfortable existence; it was also more varied and exciting. Sometimes raiders would come from the hostile folk beyond the passes and carry off his plough oxen. It might even happen that two armies met and fought a pitched battle in a neighbouring meadow. Or an enemy would invade the countryside in force, driving him and the rest of the country people with all their portable goods within the shelter of the city walls. There he would huddle along with the others, a homeless insanitary crowd, eating garlic and chervil, staring at the smoke on the horizon which told that the foe was burning their steadings and vine-props, hewing down their fruit trees, trampling under foot the young wheat, choking up the well 'with the bed of wild violets at the edge'. When the invaders withdrew, the country folk, or those of them who had survived the plague and famine of the siege, went back to their ruined homes filled with that strange passion which makes it impossible for the most unsuccessful and toil-broken farmer to take a permanent interest in anything except the tilling of the soil. There they could begin the old life over again away from the town with its godless Sophists, its pestilential Informers, and all those ridiculous Orators, who understood nothing, just nothing, about the 'land'.

The life of the farmer must at all times move in harmony with the recurrent seasons. It is this which gives it a poetry of its own in spite of its hardships and its monotony. The Greek farmer marked eagerly the first signs of spring. The most infallible perhaps was the coming of the swallows. A Greek vase has got the inscription : "*Look, there's a swallow!*" "*So it is, by Heracles!*" "*Spring is come!*" It is better however, Hesiod warns, to have your vines pruned *before* the shrill note of 'Pandion's daughter' is heard in 'the whitening spring'. Then you will be on the safe side, and not feel that Time has stolen a march on you when one of the farm lads runs to say he has just heard 'a cuckoo cuckooing' in an oak. After that, things grow at a wonderful rate, especially if there has been a suitable rainfall, which is just as much as will fill the footprint of an ox in the mould. Soon the leaves on the top branches of the figtrees are as big as a crow's foot. If you live near the sea, you may now venture to take down the rudder which has been hanging all winter above the fire, and launch your boat; that is, if you are reckless and avaricious enough to tempt Providence in that way. It is much better to stay quietly on shore, and watch the coming of the windflowers and crocuses and the hyacinth-like asphodel that shoots up the height of a man's waist, and the blossoming of the figtree and the appletree, and the scarlet flowers of the pomegranate. There will be plenty to do in the vineyard picking the slugs from the young leaves and chasing away the goats, and in the fields weeding out the darnel and agrimony, the violets and the wild tulips, from the just appearing wheat.

Then follows the long, hot, rainless summer; for Greece has a brief spring and no autumn at all. Soon everything begins to look parched and brown. The vine leaves begin to bronze and curl, and the grape clusters to form. When they begin to ripen, you must employ a boy to sit on the vineyard wall and scare away the birds. And you had better keep an eye on him yourself, or very likely he will fall to making a locust-cage out of rushes, and never notice a fox that may have got in among the vine rows. The birds are a great nuisance in the orchard also, birds and insects, whole swarms of them. The birds eat the white sesame seed and the poppy seed and the myrtle berries, and peck at the mint-leaves. When they see you coming they fly off a little distance to the flowering shrub that hides the wooden image of the garden-god, and wait there impudently till your back is turned. The insects chiefly destroy the figs. . . . It is getting abominably hot. The dry pods of the furze are bursting in the sun. The very lizards are asleep on the stone wall where the wild roses grow. Only the bees keep humming about the hollow oak and the carcass of the dead bull; and the cicala is like to drive one distracted. Let us stop work for one day and have a picnic. I know of a shady place beside a little stream that never runs dry. You get the fresh west wind in your face there. Let us take with us something good to eat—flesh and wine and honeycombs. Mallows and asphodel and edible thistles are well enough in their way and highly salubrious. But it must be admitted that they pall occasionally ; and so does cheese, and onions. It will be pleasant watching the goats feeding on the cytisus in the stony *Phelleus*. We can give the goatherd some figs and a drink of our wine, if he comes up to us in his hairy coat smelling of rennet. Perhaps he will play something to us on his reed pipe. If we do not take a holiday now, we shall not have the chance of another for a long time, now that the corn harvest and the vintage are almost upon us.

When you notice that snails are leaving the ground and crawling up plants, you know that it is time to begin the harvest. That is a long, laborious task. The corn must be cut with sickles. The fruit must be gathered and stored. The grapes must be trodden in the winepress. When it is all over there will be a Harvest Home at the farmhouse. The neighbours will come, and we shall lie down beneath an elm on beds of rushes and fresh-cut vineleaves. Apples and pears will be tumbling about us in all directions. The twigs of the damson trees will be bent under the weight of the damsons. Also there will be wine, an old and wonderful wine. There we shall lie listening to the larks and the finches and the turtles. Perhaps we shall hear a tree-frog croaking somewhere in the thorn brake; and of course the bees and the cicalas.

That will be almost the last good day. Next morning perhaps you will hear a peculiar sound and, looking up, see at a great height the long irregular wedge of the cranes on their way to Libya. That means the end of the summer. Very soon, and without other warning than the cranes give, comes a violent storm of wind and rain.   That abates, and then the ploughing must begin ; and after that the seed must be sown.   The weather is now thoroughly broken, so that you are sometimes obliged to bid the maid call in the slave Manes from the vineyard ; it is quite useless attempting to strip off the vineleaves and grubbing about the roots when the ground is soaking wet.   Let us make the best of a bad business and call in a neighbour or two and have a feast of kidney beans and figs.   There is also a thrush, and a brace of siskins, and a hare (unless the cat has stolen it).   Wine of course we must have. . . . After all, this rain is the very thing we need for the crops. We are quite justified in indulging ourselves a little.   In a week or two we shall have the opportunity of showing our gratitude to the god at the *Rural Dionysia.*   That we will certainly hold, even if our procession has to be a very small one.   Every farmer can at least marshal his own household.   He can carry the big pot himself. His daughter can carry the sacred basket on her head. The slaves can carry the pole with the *phallus* upon it. The farmer's wife can look on from the roof of the house.   We shall sing the hymn to Phales, and have a good old-fashioned *kômos.*

We shall then be in better heart to face the days when the wind blows so pitilessly cold from the snowy mountains of Thrace.   What a wind !   It sets the old men trotting to keep their blood in circulation.   It simply takes the skin off the ox—blows clean through his hide.   The goats suffer too ; but not the sheep, if their fleece is thick enough.   The woods bend and roar in the gale.   The wild creatures who live there shiver and slink from covert to covert with their tails between their legs.   It goes hard with them.   How must it go with the cuttlefish in the fireless parlour where he lives, the 'boneless one', the 'many-footed'? When you go out—and it is only little girls who may stay indoors all day—you must put on a long tunic and a thick cloak and padded sandals and a felt cap which you can pull down well over your ears. You will start game in all sorts of unlikely places and see them scurrying off on three legs. Or you may pass a number of deer huddling together in a cave.—But this weather cannot last.

So far I have given the attractive side of the picture, inventing no important detail but borrowing everything from Greek originals. It is so attractive that one is a little reluctant to give the other side. Yet it must be given, or the picture will be incomplete. It is the more important to give it owing to the tendency of a long tradition of poets and romance-writers—yes and philosophers as well—to slur it over and pretend that it does not exist. We want to know something of the misery which makes Achilles in Homer regard the lot of the labourer on a little farm as the hardest upon earth. And something may be learned. We can gather a good deal from the religion of the countryside. We can ascertain certain undoubted facts from history :—the dreadful conditions which led to the Reforms of Solon ; the ravages of the Peloponnesian War when year after year, and sometimes twice in a year, the prosperous tillage of Attica and the Megarid was devastated. And there is much that is illuminating in Hesiod, if we use his evidence circumspectly. The very conventionality of his sentiments helps us, for they are traditional and representative. What Hesiod felt was felt throughout rural Boeotia and generally throughout rural Greece.

We find in him both optimism and pessimism.   Both are conventionally expressed, but the pessimism is the more sincere.   Or perhaps it would be fairer to say that the pessimism is the more immediate reaction to the harsh surroundings which his optimism implies as much as his pessimism.   His philosophy amounts to this: ' The righteous man prospers, yes ; but he must prove his righteousness by working his fingers to the bone '. Or in his own language : 'Whoso are righteous and deal not in crooked judgements, their city flourishes and Peace the Nursing Mother of the Young dwells in the land.   For them the earth brings forth abundantly, their sheep are bowed under the weight of their fleeces, their wives bear children like their parents.   Such men will not voyage upon ships ! '   This is pure folk-philosophy, rooted in the immemorial belief that righteousness or ' justice ' has some magical efficacy inherent in it, while ' injustice ' or sin blasts the fruits of earth and man.   We know the kind of life which makes men hug a faith like that.   *I have been young, and now am old ; yet have I not seen the righteous forsaken, nor his seed begging bread.*   What can one say in answer except that it is such a pity the beautiful words have no relation to the facts ?

Hesiod knew the facts as well as any.   He said that he was living in an Iron Age, and wished that he had died earlier or that his birth had been postponed. For now men will never cease from labour and sorrow by day nor yet by night.   There will be dissension between parents and children, between guest and host, between comrades and between brethren—not as in the old days.   The young will dishonour and neglect the old, and the old revile the young.   The honest man will be held in no regard, but the unrighteous in great honour.   Might will be Right, and Pity and Indignation fly up to heaven. . . .   The poet speaks in the future tense ; things have not yet quite come to this pass. But they are hastening thither.   *The Earth is full of Plagues and full the Sea*, he says, quoting an ancient mystic sentence.   The only remedy in a world so evil is work.   'Work, foolish Perses !   There is no shame in working ; the shame is in not working '—an excellent saying.   This is not so excellent :—"There are two Spirits of Striving, an evil and a good.   The good Spirit is that which spurs a man to contend with his neighbour in the gathering of substance '.   In Hesiod's eyes, one fears, the poor in a loomp is bad.   You would not be poor if you were ' just ' and worked hard. But if you insist on wasting time at the blacksmith's forge, dropping in on a winter day for a chat with the other men who are sure to be there for the sake of the warmth, you know what to expect.   Some day you will have nothing and starve.   You will sit ' squeezing a swollen foot with a thin hand ', as the poet expresses it in a phrase quite shocking in its realism ; swollen ankles being one of the symptoms of famine.

As for Askra, where Hesiod lived, it is ' a wretched parish, bad in the winter, hard to work in the summer, excellent at no time '.   A characteristic farmer's grumble.

He is full of bitter, cynical maxims.   ' Money is the breath of life to wretched mortals '.   ' You wouldn't lose a cow but for bad neighbours '.   ' Laughingly demand a witness from your own brother '.   ' Potter is spiteful against potter, and carpenter against carpenter ; beggar is envious of beggar, and bard of bard '.   ' The shin is farther off than the knee '.   These are not individual opinions of course, but proverbs naturally arising in a certain type of society. It is a society delighting in a clumsy kind of satire against women, which may have something to do with the belief, widespread among primitive peoples, that women have no souls. An old poet, Semonides of Amorgus, wrote a poem explaining that women were really pigs and cats and foxes and other animals in human form. What Hesiod says is that Hephaestus at the bidding of Zeus fashioned out of wet earth a girl beautiful as an immortal goddess. Athena and Aphrodite gave her all gifts and all graces to inspire 'the passion that hurts and languorous broodings'; but Hermes gave her 'a shameless mind and a guileful nature'. She was called *Pandora* because all the gods bestowed gifts upon her. But every gift was a curse to man. Before she came upon earth, mankind lived free from sorrow. But she brought a great jar with her full of all manner of plagues, and opened the jar and let out the plagues, all except Hope, which stuck in the lid. And now every sort of evil roams up and down the earth. 'Trust a woman, trust a cheat', says Hesiod; and he has the Biblical warning against the strange woman. His views upon marriage are unsentimental. After all, he thinks, you cannot work a farm without a wife. The three prime requisites of the farmer are 'a house, a wife, and a plough-ox'. Best marry about thirty, but see to it that your bride is very young 'in order that you may teach her proper behaviour'—presumably the behaviour *you* deem proper. And let your choice be a neighbour's daughter, 'looking all round you carefully, in case you should marry a joke to the countryside'. Nothing is worse than a bad wife. She 'licks up your dinner' and 'singes a man without a fiery stick'. On the other hand, it must be admitted that nothing is better than a good wife. It is all very unromantic ; not like the words of Nausicaa to Odysseus : 'There is nothing higher or nobler than when man and wife are heart in heart at home'. There were no Nausicaas in Boeotia.

Who are the gods of the country ? Demeter and her daughter Persephone, Hermes and the Graces—these are perhaps the most characteristic. Dionysus is as much of the mountains as of the vineyards. Artemis and Pan are clearly more at home in the desert than in the sown. Obscenely imaged deities like Priapus and Phales and the Eros of Thespiae were apparently worshipped a good deal with that mixture of purity of heart and filthiness of act and speech which perplexes us so much in the religions we used to call 'pagan'. The most influential of the rural cults, as it was one of the oldest and most deeply rooted, was the worship of the Mother-Maid Demeter-Persephone, one goddess with a double aspect which has projected two distinct personalities. In one aspect she is the Mother and is called Demeter ; in the other she is the Maiden and called Korê or Persephone. Demeter probably means just 'Mother Earth'. Her name explains her nature well enough. But she is more distinctively the mother of corn and fruits than, like many other of the Earth-goddesses, of beasts tame and wild. After the autumn she withers and grows old. In the spring she comes up the young unravished Korê. Every spring a ritual was enacted called the Coming Up or Calling Up of Korê. It is a frequent subject of Greek art. Satyrs strike with pickaxes at a mound of earth through which, as if the mound were transparent, the head of a divine woman is seen arising. Other satyrs are dancing and manifesting a joyful surprise. This is the scene which the mummery aimed at reproducing. We hear also of the Coming Up of Semelê. Semelê, the mother of Dionysus, was essentially similar to Demeter-Korê; her name too means 'Earth'. A fragment of Pindar speaks of the worshipping multitude with pansies and roses in their hair 'when the chamber of the crimson-garmented Hours is flung open, and nectarous flowers induct the odorous Spring', and the singing and piping as they dance, beating the ground and calling upon Semelê.

This is the Greece with which Keats fell in love. We are all in love with it. Part of the extraordinary fascination which the study of Greek religion possesses for the student is that at every turn he is coming upon some accidentally recorded ritual which is a perfect symphony of flowers and fruits and music and dancing and intent young faces. But the setting of the ritual may easily delude us concerning its real character. That is as often sombre and sad as it is hilarious. Indeed in the most complete and characteristic type of ritual in the old agricultural religion the joy and the sorrow go together. An outburst of grief is followed by an explosion of delight. The god dies and the god comes to life again. It is only a very one-sided view of a very little portion of the evidence which could leave us with the impression that the Greeks were "never sick or sorry".

The truth, I imagine, is that the Greeks in their religion, as in everything else they made, aimed at a mean between the extravagances on either side. That religion was in the main a development of the primeval worship of the Dying and Reviving God which survived with much of its original character in the orgiastic cults of Asia. But the development had been in the direction of restraint and 'Sophrosynê'. The Greeks were a naturally religious people; but they would not cry out and cut themselves with knives to prove it. Neither did they deal much in hellfire and promises of everlasting pleasures. There were indeed the votaries of Orpheus, who believed in a future life, and in Heaven and Hell, and a 'personal immortality'. But the Orphics, although they had an immense influence on Greek life and philosophy, were always in a minority, as the mystic always will be. The opinion of the average Greek about death was Mr. Petulengro's; that when a man dies he is cast into the earth, and there is an end of the matter; meanwhile life is sweet, with night and day, sun, moon and stars, all sweet things, and likewise a wind on the heath. It is a Bucolic poet who sings that mallow and parsley and anise are born anew in the spring of the year, while for man, the tall and strong and wise, there is no second birth, only an unawakening sleep. Homer himself calls man the most miserable of the animals. That is not a dramatic but a popular sentiment. The lot of the common people in ancient Greece had alleviations impossible in a modern industrial community, but for all these it was bitter hard. It is sentimentality to pretend otherwise. Life was perhaps especially difficult for the tiller of the soil. He had hard work and few enjoyments. He was poorer, and lived on a sparer diet, than most of our tramps. It was easy to fall into debt and come under the power of another man. Above all, life was insecure. At any time an invasion might come, or a showerless spring, and ruin him.   All this saddened his outlook on things. He was, not in the legal but in the spiritual sense, *adstrictus glebae*, 'bound to the soil'.   He was too troubled and too tired to lift his eyes to those unsympathetic Immortals on their shining Olympus. To them he gave only a perfunctory worship.   His heart turned instinctively to the Powers that he felt to be older and nearer to humanity : the kindly ghosts of his fathers, buried prophets who being dead yet spake, and the workers of magic.

He believed in all manner of signs and omens and lucky and unlucky days. His life was guided or hampered by a number of traditional taboos. You must not cross a stream without praying and washing your hands—rather a beautiful custom, I think. You must never put the wine-ladle on the top of the mixing-bowl. You must not set a child of twelve years or twelve months—'the one thing is as bad as the other' —upon anything that will not move. He was full of superstitions about birds and beasts.   They live longer than we. 'The cawing crow lives nine genera-tions of men grown old ; the stag lives four lives of a crow ; the raven comes to his old age after three lives of a stag'.   They are wise, being old ; and especially the birds are wise.   They know all the signs of the weather. The man will prosper who lives 'marking birds and not overstepping the Law', that is, the taboos we spoke of. Truly the birds are old.   They were 'before the Titans and the Gods'.   Once upon a time 'the woodpecker was king'. They give us a deal of trouble no doubt plundering our orchards and gobbling up the seed at the very heels of the sower. Yet they keep something of their ancient sanctity and magical powers. There is the wryneck, for example, which a girl will bind upon a wheel, turning it and murmuring *Wryneck, draw him! Wryneck, draw him!*, and sure enough her lover returns to her. Then there are the snakes. They are uncanny and fearsome enough, and had better be placated with a mess of honey. But undoubtedly the souls of Heroes have entered into them. Who knows their power and their wisdom?

Spirits of all kinds are abroad. They are in the air and upon the earth. If they were not invisible, we should see them walking up and down the roads of the world. There are the kindly spirits who keep unseen guard over us, thirty thousand of them. But the *Kêres*, the hurtful spirits, are even more numerous, and the air is literally packed with them. Fixing up a sacred bough above the door, or chewing buckthorn, helps to keep them at a distance. Some even of the Heroes are dangerous and malicious beings, very devils 'the colour of a blue-bottle fly', and with rake-like teeth. Many of these—it is difficult to know just what to call them, Daemons or Heroes or even Gods—are in known graves, where we can feed them with blood, or in holes in the earth, where we can visit them and be initiated into marvellous sights. Some have dream-oracles, where we may have dreams that will bring cure to the sick body or soul, if they are rightly interpreted by the priests of the sanctuary. In the woods and wild places are satyrs and Sileni, who are ready to molest the girl who goes with her pitcher to the forest well; and the Nymphs, who rob a man of all interest in ordinary matters. Pan himself, the homely god whose image Arcadian boys flagellate with squills, will sometimes send a sudden screaming terror upon the lonely shepherd.

Against all such perils a wise man will use spells and charms and countercharms. If any one casts the evil eye upon you, spit three times into your bosom. If the menace is greater than you can deal with unaided, you may apply to the Thessalian witch who gathers virtuous herbs under the moon and can sing her down from the sky. The betrayed woman makes a waxen image of her lover and melts it before the fire, that he may melt in like manner before the fire of love; and burns barley and laurel-leaves and bran, that his flesh and bones may be consumed like that. Meanwhile she pours out prayers and libations to Hecate; and grows afraid at her own madness when she hears the dogs suddenly bay, as if they felt the approach of the dreadful goddess who walks over the graves of the dead. Curses too are often efficacious. A curse has been known to kill a man. Still there is not much satisfaction to be got out of such proceedings. It was better in the days when Cronus was king and the untilled earth brought forth all things abundantly, and the rivers ran milk and wine, and there was no war, and men did not tempt the sea in ships. But now we are fallen on an iron time.

The earth is full of ills and full the sea.

From a quite early time there were certain forces in Greek life and literature which tended to idealize the life of the rustic. One of these was Comedy. The reason is somewhat curious. Greek Comedy arose in the country or at any rate in a festival borrowed from the country. It was a development of the songs sung at the *Rural Dionysia,* the yearly festivities in honour of Dionysus held in the rural districts. In these songs the god was honoured by recounting the blessings he bestowed upon his worshippers. Thus the celebration of the *joys* of country life was a tradition in Comedy, and the rule which insisted on this at the same time debarred the poet from giving the other side of the picture. For that would have been alien to the true spirit of Comedy, which was in fact nothing but the spirit of the old ritual, where fun certainly predominated. The consequence is that the comic poets are misleading on this subject. Everything is rose-coloured. Only the vivid sense of actuality which mingles so strangely with the fantastic element in his genius saves even Aristophanes' descriptions of the country from unreality. He makes them very real, so far as they go. But he does not tell us the *miseries* of country life.

This tradition of Comedy was reinforced by the tradition of Bucolic Poetry in Greece. The origin of the pastoral poem is exceedingly obscure. But by the time of Theocritus it is clear that these Sicilian shepherds with their pretty names like Daphnis and Meliboeus and their songs about an impossible Arcady are the creations of a sentimental romanticism. This is none the less true because Theocritus knows the country and is full of natural touches, just as Aristophanes is. His poems were called Idylls, and it is the Idylls of Theocritus and his follower Virgil which have suggested the modern use of the word 'idyllic'. Country life as described by Theocritus and his successors is an idyll.

The history of Bucolic poetry is to some extent interwoven with the history of the Greek Romance which is defined for us in this context as a story with the love interest predominant. It is probable that the *Kalykê* and *Rhadina* of Stesichorus would be regarded as romances in verse if we possessed them ; but they are lost. The story of Rhadina of Corinth was taken by Stesichorus from popular tradition ; and that reminds us that the romance is really a form of popular literature, as its history in medieval and modern times shows very clearly. Popular taste craves an idyllic setting for a story of sentiment. So the Greek Romance found its natural home in Arcadia, the Arcadia of Theocritus and Sir Philip Sidney. The pastoral tale of *Daphnis and Chloe* is typical. It contains some charming episodes, and is written in a style of studied, slightly affected, simplicity. *Daphnis and Chloe* has had an immense influence, especially on French literature ; and it perhaps with Virgil's *Eclogues* was chiefly responsible for eighteenth century idealizations of country life. A generation which has read the Wessex Novels knows what to think of it.

Greek philosophy felt the attraction too. But in this case it was not the beautiful setting of rural life which attracted, but the life itself, its simplicity and austerity. The dream (born out of the very hardness of life) of a Golden Age when men were sinless and happy, and fed at a common table with the gods on the simple fruits of the earth, became something like a philosophical ideal. The Pythagoreans praised and practised the simple life. Plato is obviously attracted by it. It hardened into an absolute rule of conduct with the Cynics. It strongly affected the ideal of Stoicism and even of Epicureanism. The good man ought not to be dependent on any save himself for the satisfaction of all his needs. Other needs are superfluous and therefore sinful; for 'our basest beggars are in the poorest thing superfluous'. The contrast between the simple and the luxurious life was apt in ancient as much as in modern times to take on the character of a contrast between rural and urban life. God made the country and man made the town.

An interesting figure, who gives expression to this contrast, is Dion of Prusa called *Chrysostom* or Golden-mouthed like the more famous Christian orator, who lived much later. Dion was a Rhêtor or professional public speaker. The life of the Rhêtor was artificial to the heart. He fed upon admiration and flattery. He had the affectation of the society preacher with the vanity of an actor manager. Dion attained great eminence in his profession and was in high favour at the court of Titus. Afterwards he became involved in some affair of state and was banished from Rome by the tyrant Domitian. For a time he supported himself by the labour of his hands, wandering from place to place and mixing in the humblest ranks of society. It seems to have been a great experience for him, to have resulted in a kind of conversion. When the whirligig of Time brought in his revenges and Dion might have resumed his former position, he refused. He had definitely embraced the Cynic philosophy, and in the practice of that he felt that he had at last found his vocation. Henceforward he would have no more to do with the great ones of the earth, for he had discovered that Virtue dwells with the poor and the poorest. Because of the nobleness of the man, and because of its intrinsic charm, I will here translate part of his description of an adventure which befell him in the island of Euboea during the years of his wandering.

He was making the passage from Chios in a tiny boat with some fishermen, when a storm arose and they were wrecked at the dreaded Hollows of Euboea. No lives were lost; but the crew deciding to join their fortunes with some people in the neighbourhood who were engaged in the local purple-fishing industry, Dion found himself alone and in something of a quandary. He walked along the beach keeping a look out for any ship that might be passing or riding at anchor. He walked a long distance and saw no one. Then he noticed something lying at the very edge of the sea just under a cliff. It turned out to be the body of a stag, not yet quite dead. It had obviously fallen over the cliff. After a little he fancied that he heard the barking of dogs overhead; but the dashing of the breakers in the storm made it hard to distinguish other sounds. Making his way with the utmost difficulty—for the ancients were no Alpinists, and this was a middle aged man of letters—up a steep slope, he found dogs running about hither and thither as they do when they are at fault.   In a moment he came upon the hunter himself, who questioned him about the stag. Between them they retrieved the carcase from the sea, and Dion was invited to taste the venison at the hunter's house, which was not far away. The invitation was accepted gratefully. 'I had no fear' (our traveller says) 'of any design against me, who had nothing but a cheap cloak. And it was my experience then, as it has been my experience on many another similar occasion (for I have been a restless wanderer), that poverty is indeed a holy and inviolate thing, and the poor man far safer from outrage than official persons with all their paraphernalia.'

On their way the companions talked of the hunter's affairs and the manner of his life with his wife and children. " There are two of us, stranger, living in the same place. We are married to sisters, and have sons and daughters. We live by hunting for the most part, but we also work a little upon the land. The holding is not our own ; neither our fathers nor ourselves purchased it. Our fathers were free men indeed, but as poor as their sons, and hired themselves out to pasture the cattle of a rich man of this island who had many herds both of horses and of cattle, many flocks of sheep, and many fine fields, and much substance beside, and all these hills. But he died, and his property was confiscated. They say he was put to death by the king for the sake of his wealth. They at once drove off his cattle to be slaughtered along with some poor beasts of our own, for which we were never paid. We were then forced to stay on the spot where we had our cows and had put up some huts and a byre, built of logs and neither large nor strong, for the calves, in view of the summer, you understand ? For during the winter we fed the cattle in the valleys, where there was plenty of pasturage and large stores of fodder ; while in the summer we drove them back to the hills. Our fathers generally took up their quarters at the place we are going to. It is a watershed with a deep shady ravine through which runs a gentle stream that can be entered without difficulty by the cows, and the calves as well. It provides plenty of clean water, for its source is not far off. In summer there is always a breeze blowing through the ravine. The coppices which surround it are luxuriant and well watered, and do not breed the gadfly ; nor are they at all injurious to the cattle in any other way. There are many splendid meadows clothed with tall trees standing well apart, and there is an abundance of rich feeding all through the summer, so that the beasts did not wander very far. For these reasons they usually stalled their cattle there.

" In those days then they stayed in their cabins till they got some employment, living on the produce of a tiny piece of ground, which they had put into a state of cultivation. The steading was quite near, so that there was any amount of manure. This plot supplied all their wants. When they had time to spare from tending the cattle, they turned to hunting, sometimes with dogs, sometimes on their own account. For once two shepherd dogs, who had lost sight of the others, had turned aside to our place, leaving their charge. The first time our fathers hunted with them, they did not understand. Whenever they saw a wolf they chased it a bit, but they paid no attention to deer or wild boars. However, after tasting the blood of these creatures and often eating their flesh, they gave up the notions they had held so long, and began to prefer game to barley cakes. For getting as much as they could eat when anything was caught, and going hungry when they caught nothing, they now turned their attention more to hunting, and used to chase everything alike that showed itself, observing the scent and track of the animal, with the result that from shepherd dogs they became hunting dogs in the slow, late-learning way I have described. When winter came, there was no prospect of work for the men either down in the city or in a village. So they stopped the leaks in their cabins more carefully, and strengthened the farm buildings ; and so passed the time cultivating the piece of ground I told you about, and hunting. In the winter hunting became easier. The tracks of game are more visible, as they are imprinted on the wet soil, while the snow betrays them quite clearly, so that there is no bother searching, because you are led straight to them. Moreover the animals themselves are more disposed to cower and await the hunter. There are chances beside of catching hares and gazelles in their formes. Accordingly from that time forward they stayed where they were, quite satisfied with the life they were leading. And each married his daughter to the son of the other. And they both died just the other day almost, counting the long tale of their years, and still strong, hearty men. And my mother is still alive."

Dion's companion next tells of a visit he had paid to the city. He had been there twice in his life ; his brother-in-law, who was fifty, had never been at all. The occasion of the visit was the appearance one day of an officer from the city with a demand for money and a summons to follow him. The hunter accompanied him to town, and was conducted before certain magistrates by the messenger, who said with a smile " This is the man you sent me to. He has got nothing but his long hair and a stout log-cabin ". The magistrates then proceeded to the theatre, followed by the hunter. After some other public business had been transacted amid a babel of contending factions, the hunter was brought forward, and a debate followed. It is very vividly and amusingly described. First one orator stood up and charged the hunter and his relations with occupying land which belonged to the state without paying rent or discharging any public burden whatsoever. At the same time he accused him of being a wrecker. This speaker was followed by another, who took the line that anyone who cultivated untilled land, of which there were great stretches in Euboea owing to the depopulation of the country side, was deserving of commendation rather than punishment. Still he was of opinion that the hunter ought henceforward to pay a fair rent. Or, if he and his companions liked to buy the land outright, it should be sold them at a reduced price.

Ultimately the hunter was bidden speak for himself.

'" And what am I to say?" said I. " Speak in answer to the charge", said somebody in the audience. " Well", said I, " I tell you there is not a word of truth in what my accuser has said. Sirs, I thought I must be dreaming when I heard his nonsense about ' ploughlands' and ' villages' and the like. We have neither a village nor horses nor donkeys nor cows. I only wish we had all the nice things the gentleman spoke about, so that we might have shared them with you, and been rich folks ourselves. As it is, what we have at present is just enough for our needs ; you are welcome to any share of it you desire. Or if you want the whole of it, we shall get more." They cheered this. Then the presiding magistrate asked what we should be able to give the state. Said I, " Four magnificent deerskins". Most of the audience laughed. But the Chairman lost his temper. " Well," said I," the bearskins are hard, and the goatskins are worth less than the deerskins. But we have some more deerskins, only either old or small. You may take them as well, if you like". This annoyed him too, and he declared that I was a perfect boor from the ploughlands. " Ploughlands again !" said I. " Are you too speaking about them? Don't you hear me saying we have got nothing of the sort?"

'He asked if we would give an Attic talent each. I said "We don't *weigh* the meat[1] ; but we are ready to give what we have. A little of it is in salt. The rest is smoked—hams, venison, and other capital pieces of meat, nearly as good as the salted."

'At this there was an uproar, and they said that I was lying. The Chairman asked me if we had grain, and if so, how much. I told him the exact truth. "Three bushels of wheat, five of barley, and five of millet, and a gallon of beans—there was no crop of them this year. So take you the wheat and the barley", I said, "and leave us the millet. But if you want the millet, take it as well." "Don't you make wine too?" another man asked. "We do", said I. "And if any of you visits us we shall give him some. But he will have to bring a skin with him, for we have not got one." "How many vines have you got?" "There are the two before the door, and twenty inside the yard, and twenty again on the other side of the river, which we planted quite lately. Splendid vines they are, and bear enormous clusters when the passers by leave them alone. And that you may not be put to the bother of asking every question, I will mention to you everything else we possess : eight she goats, a hornless cow with a capital little calf belonging to her, four sickles, four mattocks, three spears, and a hunting knife each. I need not describe our crockery? We have got wives and children, and we live in two fine cabins, and have a third where we store our victuals and skins."

[1] To the hunter the talent is, what it was originally, a measure of weight, not of value.

'" Ay ", said the orator, " and where you bury your money, no doubt." " Come and dig it up, then, stupid ", said I. " Who buries *money*? It isn't a plant, I'm sure." Here everybody laughed—evidently at the orator." '

The hunter then explained to the meeting that he was a 'citizen', as his father had been before him, and that his sons and he were prepared to make any sacrifice required of them by their fellow-citizens. It was an outrage to call him a wrecker. On the contrary he was full of pity for the mariners shipwrecked on the wild coast near which he lived.

At this point there was a 'scene'. A man stood up in the audience and begged leave to make a statement. He and another man—at this the other man stood up also—had once been cast ashore on that very coast. Only a few were saved from the wreck. Those who had money were picked up by the purple-fishers. The speaker and his friend wandered, half clad and nearly dead with hunger and thirst, along a sort of path, by which they hoped to come upon some shelter occupied by neatherds or shepherds. With difficulty they reached some huts, and began to shout. " Then the hunter here came up to us, and brought us indoors, and set a fire blazing, not all at once but by degrees. He himself rubbed one of us, and his wife the other, with tallow; for they had no oil. Finally they poured warm water over us, until we had recovered from the chill. Then they made us lie down and, after wrapping us up in the best way they could, set wheaten loaves before us, while they themselves ate boiled millet. They also gave us plenty of venison both roast and boiled, and wine to drink, taking water themselves.

On our preparing to go away next day, they kept us three days longer. They then convoyed us down to the Plain, and at our leave-taking they presented us with meat and a fine skin for each. And noticing that I was still in a poor way after the hardships I had gone through, the hunter wrapped me in a little tunic which he took from his daughter, who fastened some rag or other about her instead. This, when I had got to the village, I returned. Thus we at any rate owed our lives under God chiefly to this man."

An appeal to humanitarian sentiments was as effective with a Greek as with an American audience. The theatre resounded with applause. The orator who had spoken second now saw his chance and came forward with the proposal that the hunter should be suitably rewarded at the public expense. He was presented with a tunic and a cloak and a considerable sum of money. The money he declined, but the garments were forced upon him. It was also voted that he and his children should sit rent free on their piece of land. From that time forward no one had molested them.

The hunter had just finished the story of his visit to the city, when Dion and he arrived at the cabins. Dion laughed and said, " Well, there *was* one thing you concealed from the citizens, and that the finest of all your possessions ". " What's that ? " " This garden here, which is a very fine one, and contains plenty of vegetables and fruit-trees." " We did not have it at that time, we made it later."

Dion goes on :—

' We entered, and proceeded to enjoy ourselves for the rest of the day. I reclined upon leaves and skins spread on a high pallet. The hunter sat, his wife by his side.   A marriageable daughter waited upon us and filled up our cups with a sweet dark wine. The servants prepared the meat and laid the dishes, and themselves dined with the family, so that I thought with admiration of these folk and considered them the happiest people I had ever known. Yet I had known the houses and tables of rich men, not only private citizens, but great nobles and potentates. And now the impression I had previously formed of the unhappiness of the great was most strikingly confirmed when I observed the poverty and frankness of my hosts, who enjoyed the pleasures of eating and drinking just as much or even more.

'While we were thus having a good time of it, the other hunter came in. He was accompanied by his son, a spirited lad, who was carrying a hare. The boy blushed as he entered. While his father was embracing me, he kissed the girl and presented her with the hare. She then stopped serving us, and sat down beside her mother, while the lad waited upon us in her place. I then asked my host "Is this the young lady from whom you took the tunic you gave to the shipwrecked man?" "No", he replied with a smile, "the one you mean was married to a rich man in the village long ago and has a family of her own, well grown children." "So you have all you need?" "We lack for nothing", said my hostess, "and they get something when any game is caught, and fruit and vegetables—for they haven't a garden. This year we got wheat from them, just the seed, and we paid them back at once when harvest came." "Well", said I, "and do you intend to marry your daughter here to another rich man, so that she also may lend you wheat seed?"

'But at this the boy and girl both blushed. Her father said "She will get a poor man like ourselves, a hunter", and looked in the direction of the young man with a smile. And I: "Why do you not marry her at once? Must the husband come from some village?" "I have a notion that he is not far away. In fact he is in this very house. And we shall have the wedding to be sure when we have chosen a suitable day." "How do you decide that a day is suitable?" "The moon must be of a good size, and the atmosphere clear; a fine moonlight night." "Well now, is he really a good hunter?" "I can tire out a stag and stand up to a wild boar", said the young man. "You will see for yourself to-morrow if you like, stranger." "And was it you who caught this hare?" "Yes", he said with a laugh, "I caught it with the snare during the night. . . . It was the most beautiful clear weather and there was the biggest moon that ever was seen." Here the two fathers burst out laughing, and the young man fell into an abashed silence. So the maid's father said "It isn't me, my boy, that is responsible for the delay. But your father is waiting until he can go and buy a victim. For you must sacrifice to the gods." At this the girl's younger brother said "Why, he has had a victim ready for quite a time. It is here on the farm and is being kept at the back of the house—a fine beast." "Really?" they asked the young man. "Yes." "How on earth did you come by it?" "When we caught the wild sow with the young ones I hit one of them with a stone, and threw my skin-coat over it when it was caught. The rest made off in all directions; they ran faster than the hare. But I exchanged the one I caught for a young pig in the village, and made a stye behind the house, and reared the hog there." "So this was what made your mother laugh whenever I wondered at hearing a pig grunt, and why you used up so much of the barley!" "You see, the chestnuts were not enough to fatten her; she did not care even for acorns. But if you would like to see her, I shall go and fetch her." They bade him do so. Off they ran on the spot, he and the slave lads, in high glee.

'Meanwhile the girl rose and brought from the other cabin minced service berries and medlars and winter apples and swelling clusters from the generous grape bunch, and set them on the table, wiping it with leaves after the meat course, and putting everything upon clean ferns. Also the boys now came bringing the pig with laughter and sport. They were accompanied by the lad's mother and his two little brothers carrying loaves of pure wheat, and boiled eggs in wooden trenchers, and roasted chickpeas. After embracing her brother and her niece she sat down beside her husband and said "There is the victim; our son has been keeping it for some time against the wedding. We have made all the other preparations as well, and the wheaten flour and barley meal are ready. The only other thing we shall need, I think, is a drop of wine, and that can easily be got from the village." Her son stood close beside her with his eyes fixed upon his prospective father in law, who remarked mischievously "Here is the one who can't make up his mind. Probably he wants to go on fattening his pig awhile." "She is bursting with fat", said the lad; and I, anxious to come to his rescue, said "Take care that your boy doesn't get thin while the pig is getting fat." "Our guest speaks the truth", said his mother. "You would hardly know him just now, he is so thin. Just the other day I saw him get up in the night and leave the cabin." "The dogs were barking", quoth he, "and I went out to see what for." "Nothing of the sort. You were walking about like a madman.—So don't let us allow him to suffer longer." Here she put her arms round the neck of the girl's mother and kissed her; and the latter said to her husband "Let us do as they wish". So the matter was settled, and they said "Let us have the marriage the day after to-morrow". They invited me to stay on, and I gladly consented.'

With this pleasant impression one is tempted to break off. Of course it is only half true, only one other philosophical Arcadia. So Goldsmith might have written, had he lived in the first century. Dion's story has the delicate humanity, the simple and yet cunning technique, the very sentiments of the *Deserted Village* and the *Vicar of Wakefield*. It has also got the same relation to actuality.

MOTHER AND DAUGHTER

And year by punctual year
Man laboureth the Earth,
The Unwearied and Deathless, dear
Mother that gave him birth;
When the slow ploughs come and go,
As the mule-team strains and plods,
Wounding the breast of her so,
The Eldest of Gods.

Soph. Antig. 338–341.

[*Introductory Note.*—There are two principal ways of dealing with ancient mythology. The first may be called the objective way. It is the method of the researcher analysing, arranging, and classifying his data. The second is more subjective, and is the way of the dramatist, the painter, the story-teller. The first method is concerned with the origin and growth of the material to which it is applied. The second, accepting the story as it stands, regards it purely as matter of art. The two methods are not mutually exclusive, and it is not too much to say that the twentieth century is learning to combine them. The present Study aims at doing this. It is an attempt to give form to the spirit of the Demeter myth without the use of unauthentic details, borrowing as far as possible the language of ancient writers themselves, and keeping constantly in mind the results of modern scholarship. The dramatic framework is of the slightest, and is employed simply because some kind of dramatic form, obvious or implicit, seems necessary for the just representation of a subject which is essentially dramatic, in fact the mythus or plot of an actual mystery-play.

Several versions of the story are preserved, differing greatly, but differing only, in detail. The locality and the subordinate incidents—all the local colour, as we call it—were determined by the situation of the shrine and ritual with which a particular version was connected. Thus the Attic version was connected with Eleusis, the Sicilian version with the Vale of Enna. I have not followed any actually recorded version, but have tried to extract the essential elements of them all and to harmonize their details. This is not an arbitrary, but rather a scientific, proceeding. For not only does it, if successfully carried out, give us a coherent picture, but it fixes the attention on the basic elements of the legend, which are exceedingly simple, primitive, and touching. Whereas in the *Hymn to Demeter*, for example, the human characters of the plot are not simple persons at all, but kings and queens and divinized ancestors.]

The scene is the interior of a hut in a lonely part of Greece, at the foot of a hill, just where the tillage ceases. It is a single, moderately large room, oblong in shape, without windows or a chimney. The walls are of naked sundried bricks. Driven into them here and there are a few wooden pegs, from which depend some rude garments of goatskin or coarse woollen cloth, a dried oxhide stretched upon a frame

—a shield—and a quiver with a number of short bronze-tipped arrows in it. The floor is irregularly paved with flat stones. There is scarcely any furniture. A little table, one or two chairs (uncushioned and without backs), a good deal of pottery including one great vessel in which a man could hide, some bedding at present bundled away in a corner, a spindle-and-whorl, a potter's wheel—these are the chief things. Skins of animals are disposed here and there. One notices a hunting spear and a fishing rod standing in another corner. In the middle of the room is a low circular hearth burning charcoal, which emits a dull red glow in the dim interior lit only by that and by the light admitted through the open door. The door further serves as an issue for the acrid wood-smoke, which has long since blackened the walls, and now eddies about the chine of a pig suspended by a hook from the roof. The whole effect is, by modern standards, inexpressibly bare, cheerless and uncomfortable. Yet it is better·than most houses of its kind, these being composed of rubble, or even of wattle and daub.

A young girl, clad in a single piece of cloth fastened at the shoulder by a pin like a safety pin, is parching some barley grain over the embers.

An elderly man enters carrying a dead goat. He is very wild and hairy looking, with a great beard and flowing locks. He is wearing a fleece over his undergarment.

The Man (*tossing the goat on the floor*). There! I found it on the hill, near the path, on my way home.
The Girl. Alas, how did it die?

The Man. How? From hunger of course. This is the fourth since the full moon. If a goat cannot live, what can?

The Girl (handling the goat). It is just skin and bone, there will not be much to eat. . . . Its eyes have been pecked out.

The Man. I scared away a raven. The ravens and wolves are the only creatures that fare well in these days. . . .

The Girl. Is there any sign of the rain yet?

The Man. No sign. To-day is the same as all the other days. The watercourse has been dry all the winter save for a little trickle in the bottom, and that the sour water of the hill bog. Not the smallest blade of corn has yet shown itself, although the swallows are come. How could it, when the ground is as hard as horn?

The Girl. This year we shall have a Flower Festival without any flowers. Perhaps the dead will be angry and not come. There is not a crocus or a violet to be seen.

The Man. The crocuses and violets might fare well for me, if only I saw the figblossom and the grape-blossom and the young leaves of the olives. But it is worst of all about the corn, because we need that most. I have ploughed twice, and sown five times, but it is useless. It is as if some enemy had parched the seed.

The Girl. But is it not the same everywhere?

The Man. It is the same. And we are better off than most, being rich. Have we not a field and a garden and a yoke of oxen and sheep and goats? Had we not a slave woman till she died the other day? How must it go with a man who has no possession of his own, but must labour on the field of another nearly as poor as himself?

The Girl.   They say many of that sort have died.

The Man.   It must be so.   Pestilence is the brother of Famine.   Yesterday I saw one from the village, as I suppose, sitting with his back against a boundary stone. His head hung down between his drawn-up legs, which were as sharp as ploughshares, and his hands were clutching his ankles.   I spoke to him, but he answered nothing.   I pushed him with my foot, and he fell over on his side and lay still. . . . A dog was slinking behind some shrubs.   I threw a stone at it, and it ran away ; but not far.

The Girl (*in a matter of fact tone due, not to callousness, but to her acceptance of life as a precarious thing full of near and horrible menaces*).   Did it eat him afterwards?

The Man (*in the same tone*).   I do not know.   I suppose so.   The dogs have eaten many this winter. (*Taking off his sheepskin coat and throwing it over one of the stools, on which he sits down*).   How much have we left?

The Girl.   About a bushel of wheat meal, and perhaps two bushels of barley meal, and of barley grain, and sesame.   There is also a little bag of chickpeas. A good deal of cheese is left.   And some preserved olives.   Then there is the oil, and the swine's flesh there, and half of the hare you killed yesterday, and the big jar of wine.   We have plenty of salt, but the honey is nearly done, and so are the dried onions and the figs.

The Man.   The honey harvest failed because of the rainy summer.   Who ever heard of two such evils at once—a wet summer and a rainless winter? . . . The seasons are confounded and all things turned upside down and the rivers flow back to their fountains. The race of men has doubtless committed some great impiety, and the god is wroth with us.

The Girl. If the Earth does not send up her fruits this year, who can save us?

The Man. None but a god.

> *A woman appears in the doorway. She is wrapped in a black robe, which is drawn over her head and falls to her feet. She stands silent a moment before speaking. They see that she is old.*

The Old Woman. Hail!

The Man. Hail thou also! and come in.

> *As she crosses the threshold they have the impression that she has grown suddenly tall, and that a strange light radiates from her. But, as their eyes are a little dazzled by the setting sun now shining in at the door, and as she appears an ordinary old woman again when she has stepped into the house, they imagine that they must have been mistaken.*

> *The man places for her the seat on which he has been himself sitting.*

Sit down. You look weary.

> *The old woman sits down in silence, and uncovers her head. She appears scarcely aware of their presence. There is in her face an expression of such devouring and immortal sorrow that they are awed into a respect and marvelling that is partly superstitious.*

The Man (kindly). Will you eat?

She nods refusal.

The Man. You seem old and poor. There are many like you in these days who would sell themselves or sell their children into slavery for a little bread. Are you alone of mortals able to live without bread? . . . Or do you fast from grief?
The Old Woman. From grief.
The Man. How long have you been fasting?
The Old Woman. A long time.
The Man. Do not grieve overmuch. Nothing should be done too much ; it makes the gods angry. Sorrow and death and old age must come to us all, and we must bear them as we can. There is no help in lamentation. Eat and drink and forget your trouble for a little. . . .

> *As the stranger remains unmoved, the girl approaches her and speaks.*

Will you not eat, mother? If you should die here, it will bring a curse upon the house.

> *Something in this speech causes the stranger to start from her reverie. She puts her hands on the girl's shoulders and peruses her face intently. The girl's eyes fall before the deep unwavering gaze of the other, but she is not vexed or frightened. A sensation of lightness and force seems to pass through her body from the touch of the strange old woman.*

The Old Woman. You are like someone I knew.

The Girl (with perfect simplicity). Was she as tall and beautiful as I?

The Old Woman (with equal simplicity). Much taller and more beautiful.

The Girl. Will you eat now?

The Old Woman. I will eat, because you remind me of her, and that it may be of good omen to me and to this house. But only a little mess of barley and water.

> *The girl mixes the barley and water in an earthenware pot with a wooden spoon, heating the mixture over the fire.*

The Man (conventionally). Who are you, where do come from, and who are your parents?

The Old Woman. I am the daughter of a great King, that was driven into exile.

> *Neither the man nor his daughter manifests surprise at this, for the old woman has a certain majesty about her, and they live in a world where such reversals of fortune are common.*
>
> *The mess is served in a wooden bowl, and the old woman eats without a spoon by means of a piece of bread hollowed into a cavity.*

The Man. It is likely you have suffered many things and great . . . How is it you came here?

The Old Woman. I have been wandering. . . .

The Man. Were you seeking anyone?

> *Instead of answering the stranger veils her head once more in her dark cloak. It is a sign of profound grief.*

The Man (*with awkward kindness*). Perhaps you will find whom you seek to-day or to-morrow or very soon. . . . The gods bring unexpected things to pass, and nothing is too strange for happening. . . . Others too have lost those whom they loved the most. . . . They say that a Stone Woman weeps for ever on the slope of a distant hill for her many children, her sons and her young daughters, that were slain by the wrath of gods. Your misery cannot be greater than hers, and she was half-divine. . . .

The Old Woman (*speaking slowly and as if to herself*). I had one daughter only. . . . She grew up like a blossoming branch in a well-watered place. She was so glad and so beautiful that I was half afraid, feeling like one that has a great treasure and thievish neighbours. And something in her I hardly understood made me the more afraid. Sometimes in the midst of her wonderful happiness she would suddenly turn grave and solemn, she could not tell me why. So I was afraid and hid her away in a secret valley. She used to go in the mornings with other girls to gather the wild flowers. For nowhere were such flowers to be seen as in that valley. No one ever came there but she and her companions. So I thought her safe, and departed on a journey. . . . Yet all the time my heart was troubled like a purple sea. I had a dream; and seemed to see her before me, pale and appealing, stretching out her arms. And I awoke in terror, sure that I heard her cry of ' Mother !' And I sprang from my couch, and ran out like a mad woman over the wooded hills, and sought her in the valley, crying her name everywhere, but she was not there. And from that day to this I have sought her over the world without rest, but have not found her.

The Man. I have heard of a man who was lost in strange places for ten years, and yet came home safely to his wife at last, and slew those who had devoured his substance in his absence.

The Old Woman (disregarding his words). What part of the earth have my feet not visited? I have gone from house to house, like a beggar, resting by wells and under trees. I have slept also in caves and in the open fields. Some received me kindly. Some mocked and drove me away, saying that I brought ill luck and was the cause of the famine. The children of the villages stoned me. . . . And once by the sea-shore pirates found me and carried me away in their ship; but I escaped from them. And once I was the nurse of a king's son, a young child, till his mother took him from me when I would have saved him from death, and I went away in a rage.

The Man (kindly). You need not go away from here, mother, if you wish to stay. . . . (*With unaffected self-approval*) The pious man who is kind to strangers, his house shall prosper. You shall have your share of our store as long as it lasts.

The Old Woman. May you fare well for your hospitality. But I may not rest from wandering till I reach the end of my journey.

The Man. It may be very far off. Perhaps—may it not be so!—she is no longer living.

The Old Woman. The like of her cannot die. . . .

The Man. Nay, even the nymphs die at last. . . . It may be, while you are wandering across the world, your daughter is seeking you, coming always a day too late, to find you gone before. . . . We shall not grudge you food, for you could help my little daughter here about the house in place of our old servant, who died of a disease.

The Girl (who has been feeding the fire with dry twigs and pieces of bark, which make it leap up and illumine the darkening room). Stay with us, mother, at least till you are rested. . . . What can you do, little old woman? Are you strong enough to pound the corn in the quern?

The Old Woman. I can do that, and I can bake the bread, and weave both wool and flax.

The Girl. I will gather sticks for the fire, and carry water from the well.

The Man. It is time for me to go away now. It is the lambing season, and I must spend the night on the hill tending the mothers. . . . But it is little profit. The ewes die this year and the lambs with them.

The Old Woman. We all have our sorrows.

They all begin lamenting together in a kind of high rhythmical wail.

Your sorrow comes to an end, but not mine.

The Man. Nay, mother, Death does not always stand aloof from any. . . . How old are you?

The Old Woman. As old as the Earth.

> *The Man, thinking her crazed with grief, puts about him a thick shepherd's coat, grasps a crooked stick, and goes out. The Old Woman sits brooding over the fire.*

The Girl (to herself). I wonder what she is thinking about. . . . She looks almost as old as she said. . . . Perhaps she is a little mad. But I am not afraid of her. (*Aloud*) I heard an owl hoot just now. Do you wish to lie down and sleep, mother?

The Old Woman. It is pleasant to talk beside the fire before sleep.—Tell me, how do you live here day by day?

The Girl. As you see. It is the life of the country people. Do you not know it?

The Old Woman. Who knows it, if I do not? It is my life, also.

The Girl. I have never known any other.

The Old Woman. And does it content you?

The Girl. I was content till lately. But now everything has changed and become hard and bitter. There is a curse upon the land, and nothing grows but darnel and bindweed and blue thistles ; for the corn seed withers or is picked up by the birds. My work too is harder since my fostermother died. I have to get up now before dawn and rouse the sparks in the fire, kneeling and blowing with my mouth till my face is blackened and my eyes smart with the smoke. . . . We had abundance of everything then. We were not afraid of the hunger.

The Old Woman. Are there none of your race but your father and you?

The Girl. My mother died many years ago. My brother was killed in a battle about kine. My father's brother lives in a distant village, more than a hundred stades away.

The Old Woman. Did you miss your mother?

The Girl. I did for a time. And then I forgot.

The Old Woman (*to herself*). Yes, they forget. . . .

The Girl (*seeing her shiver*). Are you cold, mother? I will bring fresh firewood from behind the door.

The Old Woman. No. It is not cold. I was only remembering something. . . . Perhaps my coming will bring you luck.

The Girl. May it be so! Then when the harvest comes we shall have the old fun again. We shall be treading the grapes with our bare feet till we are splashed from head to foot with the juice. How we used to laugh! . . . And I like shaking the figtrees till the ripe figs tumble down, and gathering the apples and pomegranates in our flat baskets. . . . Then there is the Harvest Home, when the men plant a winnowing shovel on a heap of wheat, doing honour to the goddess.

The Old Woman. Did you ever see her?

The Girl. No. It is hard to see the gods when they would not. They say she carries a bunch of corn in one hand and poppies in the other, and that she is blonde and smiling. But now, it seems, she does not come near us nor smile upon us any longer. My father says it is because of the sinfulness of men, for in the old days the gods used to visit the houses even of the poorest and eat with them from the same table. Therefore in those days the earth produced its fruits without our labour. The rivers ran with milk and wine, and the bees made honeycombs in the hollow oaks, and it was always spring. But now it is winter in the midst of spring. I have looked, and there is hardly a flower to be seen except here and there about a well or a marshy place. The irises round the lake may be beginning to flower now, but I am afraid to go there.

The Old Woman. Why?

The Girl. It is dark and lonely and strange-looking.

They say it has no bottom and is a way down to the
dead. Many stories are told of it.

The Old Woman (*thoughtfully*). What stories?

The Girl. They say that a girl was carried down
the cleft.

The Old Woman (*earnestly*). What do you say?

The Girl. I will tell you. There was a shepherd
who saw it. He came and told us. He was afraid.
He said that when he was on the hillside, looking towards the lake, it grew suddenly black as night over it.
Then he heard a great noise—trampling of horses
and rolling of wheels. That frightened him because he
knew no ordinary horses could drag a car over that
ground, and their swiftness seemed terrible. Through
all that noise he made sure that he heard the crying
of a girl. Then came a yet louder sound, louder than
thunder ; it was as if the earth had been cloven in twain.
Then came silence again, and clear sky, and no sign
of anyone, men or horses. . . . My father went with
the shepherd to the lake. They saw a breach newly
made in the rocky side of the lake, and a long trail of
flowers leading from the cleft to the meadows beyond.
He brought some of the flowers with him. There was
one I did not know. It had a strange, sweet, over-
powering smell.

The Old Woman. When was this?

The Girl. Last year.—What is wrong, mother?
You look very strangely.

The Old Woman. Which is the way to the lake?

The Girl. You follow the footpath from the door
till it enters the torrent-bed. You climb up that till
you reach the ridge of the hill, and the lake lies in the
hollow beyond the hill.

The Old Woman rises hastily from her seat. She seems filled with an unnatural force and energy.

The Girl. Are you mad, old woman? You cannot go there in the night! You will lose your way, or stumble among the stones of the torrent and be hurt.

The Old Woman. Do not hinder me, lest some evil thing befall you.

The Girl is subdued by some mysterious dignity and authority in the stranger's voice and gestures. The Old Woman seizes two pieces of resinous wood and kindles them at the fire. Then she rushes from the house holding a blazing torch in either hand. The Girl has again the illusion of gigantic stature, which she attributes to the deceptive flicker of the torch light. She follows the Old Woman to the door and gazes after her.

She is past the wild figtree. . . . Now she is crossing the brook—but it is dry now. . . . Now she is on the causeway that a king built for his treasure-waggons long ago. . . . Past the ruined chapel of the mountain goddess. . . . She has reached the untilled meadow where the lightning fell. . . . Out of sight! . . . Certainly the old woman must be mad—or a god in disguise?

A breath of wind, sighing as if it came from a great distance, lifts her hair softly. She shivers a little, shuts the door and fastens it, somewhat hastily. She comes back slowly to the fire. She kneels and builds it up in such a way that it will smoulder a long time.

She started when I spoke of the maid that was lost at the lake. . . . I understand now! She thought it was her daughter whom she is looking for, and has gone to seek her there. . . . What is the good of looking for her now? It is many months since the earthquake. . . . The old woman said that her daughter was very beautiful, and she herself may have been beautiful once too. . . . Shall I too marry and bear a daughter and grow old and ugly and foolish? . . . I do not feel sleepy to-night. I cannot help thinking of the strange little old woman.

She sits down at the table and leans her head upon her arms. Outside, the cry of a bird is heard. She raises her head quickly.

That was a crane! What makes it cry at night? It means something—perhaps a change in the weather.

She goes to the door, opens it, and looks out, a little timidly.

Nothing. . . . No sign of the old woman. . . . There are frogs croaking not far away. . . . I wish it were dawn, or that father would come. Then we might look for her; when two go together one sees a thing before the other. She may easily sink in the mire about the lake, like the young bull two years ago. . . . There are no stars to-night, and the moon is too young to show through the clouds. How dark it is!

A gentle rustling noise is heard. It is the coming of the rain. A drop strikes her face.

Ah!

She puts her hand out.

O joy, the rain at last! The god has had mercy upon us. Great big drops. This will save everything. . . . How it is raining! I never saw such torrents of rain. Soon the watercourse will be flooded and bellowing like a bull. I hope the old woman is not in it; else she will be swept away, it rises so suddenly. Once it drowned a swineherd boy that way. (*Shouting*) Mother, mother, come in! . . . No answer. Well, I must keep inside myself and shut the door, or the rain water will come in and get among the meal perhaps, or soak our beds.

> *She shuts the door and stops the chink between it and the ground with a strip of hide. Then she spreads a sort of mattress on the floor, at the far end of the room, opposite the door.*
>
> *Someone beats upon the door and shouts. She opens it to her father, who comes in dripping and wildly excited.*

The Man (*flinging off his sheepskin coat*). It came on all at once. What a night! The ground is drinking it all in as fast as it comes down. You can hear it drinking like a cow. The sky is full of strange noises: I was half afraid. Now that the god is sending us rain, I want to dance!

> *He goes through the rhythmical movements and gestures of a primitive dance. His daughter beats time with her hands. The whole performance seems curiously deliberate in its spontaneity, and is only saved from a ludicrous effect by a touch of solemnity. For the dance is not merely an expression of the man's joy but a ritual in honour of the god. When it is over, the Man goes to the fire to dry himself.*

The Man. Where has the stranger gone?

The Girl. She went out before the rain came on some wild errand. I think she must be a little mad. She is always dreaming of her lost daughter and hoping to find her.

The Man. How could she find anyone in the darkness?

The Girl. She took two flaming brands with her.

The Man. The rain has put them out by this time. —Which way did she go?

The Girl. She has gone to the Dark Lake.

The Man (reflectively). To the lake? . . . Strange.

The Girl. Why do you say that, father?

The Man. Because of a thing I have seen to-night. —I was tending the ewes on the farther slope of the hill. I made a fire of dry sticks and heath, and I brought the ewes into the light and warmth of the fire. It burned straight up into the air as if it were in a cave. A sheep was bleating somewhere distressfully. I found it at the foot of a rock out of the light cast by the fire. I happened to look down into the valley where the lake is. There was a magical light upon it, like a shining golden mist, and it hid the lake and the parts round. I watched it a long time, wondering. There was a great hooting of the owls that live on the banks of the water—I never saw any other birds there. And all over the countryside I heard the baying and howling of dogs.

The Girl (fearfully). That means——

The Man. Hush! It is better not to speak of these things. . . . Then I heard a voice, two voices, weeping aloud—strong, clear voices—unquenchable voices. I do not know whether they were weeping for joy or for sorrow.

The Girl.   What if the old woman——?

The Man (*solemnly*).   These were the voices of immortals.

The Girl.   What will become of her if she sees *them* against their will?

The Man.   We cannot know. . . . After a time the voices fell silent.   I noticed that the sky was full of fluttering, squeaking bats.   My father used to say that the ghosts of the dead flutter and squeak like that. There were many flashes of lightning without thunder. Certainly some marvellous thing was happening.

The Girl.   I heard a crane crying in the darkness.

The Man.   The cranes fly north in great troops through the night at this season or, rather, earlier.   It is a sign of spring.   Soon we shall hear the cuckoo calling from the evergreen oaks and sycamores.

The Girl.   I wonder if it is raining still.

She opens the door.   A faint white light comes in.

It is almost off.   The dawn is coming.

The Man.   There is more rain coming.   Enough has fallen for the time. . . . Do you hear the roaring of the torrent?

The Girl.   I wonder if the old woman is safe.

The Man.   We will go and look for her, now that the light is broadening.   It may be some lamb or kid has fallen into the flood, so we shall be looking for two things at once.—Let us put on our cloaks and go.

*They go out, leaving the door ajar; so admitting a
dim radiance which is very weak and doubtful
at first and hardly illumines the room, but
gradually strengthens, until at the end of the*

scene the whole house is flooded with the fresh light of a perfect Spring morning. Two figures enter. They would be almost invisible in that interior, if it were not for a kind of glory seeming to emanate from them rather than to be reflected upon them by the dawn or the smouldering fire. They are female, very tall, and majestic in their movements. From their appearance one judges them to be mother and daughter.

The Mother. This is the house. . . . The man and the girl have gone out. Here you may rest awhile after your long journey. You are still weak and look helplessly, almost like a new born child.

The Daughter. Yes, I would rest a little. (*Slowly*) I have come very far. . . . It was very dark, as if there was a moon somewhere, but hidden behind thick clouds. When I came into this glory, it struck my eyes like lightning.

The Mother. Yet the sun is not risen.

The Daughter. I came over great marshes and melancholy plains and slow black rivers like corrupted blood.

The Mother. Alas !

The Daughter. And other things I saw—shadowy things that drew back as I looked on them. They drove past me like dead leaves in a great wind or a migration of birds. They bore the forms of old men and children, of warriors with armour all bloody, young men and maidens unwed. The air was full of moans and of sighing, chiefly on the marges of a broad sedgy river, where the shapes were holding out their hands in a passion of longing for the farther shore. Then I understood that these were the unhappy dead who had not found burial on earth. And so they must abide on this side of that water, in those broken lights, with peace neither of body nor of mind, filled full of unsatisfied desires and unsatisfied regrets.

The Mother. It is their destiny. We too, even we the gods, must endure our destinies.

The Girl. Moreover I crossed a violent river of fire.—O I have seen things too great for tears.

The Mother. The sadness of what you have seen has passed into your eyes.

The Daughter. That may well be, mother. Because I have been in a land, not only of the dead, but as it were dead itself. There is a sun and a moon, but the sun is like a dying lamp and the moon like a white flower. There are no mountains, no torrents, and no sea; only an endless plain with here and there a grove of tall poplars or the low willows that drop their berries. No purple flowers are there—the pansy or the rose or the red anemone—only pallid blossoms, asphodel and white poppies and my own flower the narcissus. . . . The notes of the shy birds are low and few and sad. . . . The dead, wandering in the dim and mouldering land, have no hopes, but only memories.

The Mother. Here upon earth, when a mortal dies, we turn our eyes away.

The Daughter (excitedly). Ah yes! it is good to be back on the comfortable earth again, in your arms, mother! I feel like one new awakened from an evil dream.

She rises and moves about the house.

My desire is to touch and handle everything, lest it

should turn out unsubstantial like the things I have lived among so long.

She stops at the open door.

Sunlight, beautiful sunlight! I am a snake in the spring that has cast his wrinkled winter skin, a north-ward flying swan, a watered hyacinth! . . . Mother, there is nothing better for a man than to be alive— to feel the blood running sweetly in his veins, to hold the daylight in his eyes, to hear and to utter articulate human words, to have and to embrace those he loves. Even the deathless ones feel that. Alas for the echo-like voices, the forms that melt as you clasp them like vapour or smoke or dreams!

The Mother. Ah, that breaks the heart, I know! In your lost days I used to see you often in dreams, and when I stretched out my arms to embrace you, they gathered only the empty air. And when first you came up to my call, you looked so strange and pale, I thought for a moment it was but some dream of you or bodiless image of my desire. But now you gather colour like an almond tree in March.

The Daughter. I feel the Spring in my blood. And you, mother—you are like the fruitful Autumn, calm and sweet and kind, like Earth herself in the season of fruits.

The Mother. She is the mother of gods and men, and in her life we live.—When in my wrath and grief I cursed her and she withered, my own body withered and shrank, till I had the seeming of an ancient crone past the season of motherhood. Now, when her life stirs in me anew, I am as you see. For the seed of all life is in her.

The Daughter. The seed of death is in her also, mother.

The Mother. What have we to do with death, my child?

The Daughter. All men have need of the gods, men say. Have they need of us only while they are alive?

The Mother. It is men's fate to die. We cannot save them from that, nor help them after that.

The Daughter. Alas!

The Mother. It is idle bewailing what must be.

The Daughter (*as if to herself*). They stretched out their hands to me. . . .

The Mother (*reassuringly*). You will return no more where their unhappiness can vex your peace.

The Daughter. No more?

The Mother. Having lost you once, should I let you go again?

The Daughter. . . . Mother, I must go back.

The Mother. Hush, child! These are wild words. This sudden coming into the light has bewildered you —as when a torch is flashed on a sleeping man and he springs up in amazement and mutters foolish things.

The Daughter (*sadly*). Nay, I know what I say; and what I say is true.

The Mother. Who can tear you from me?

The Daughter. Destiny.

The Mother. Destiny will not hurt us till we break her law.

The Daughter. I have broken it.

The Mother (*wildly*). What do you say?

The Daughter. Listen, mother, and have pity for me. When first I was led to that dim palace of the King, I would not be persuaded to eat; for I was possessed by grief and thoughts of you. And I fasted all the time of my sojourn there till the last day. Then one put a ripe pomegranate in my hand and I, distraught and scarcely knowing what I did, put it to my lips and tasted a little of the scarlet fruit. Then a voice told me that, having eaten the food of the ghosts, my place was henceforth among them.

Thĕ Mother. Alas, alas, my child! Why did I bear you for my sorrow to such an evil destiny?

Thĕ Daughter. Nay, mother, do not weep and veil your head. Be you content as I am content.

Thĕ Mother. Content!

The Daughter. You have heard it :—if I go back, it is always to return to you again. If I must spend part of the year there, the rest of the year I shall be with you.

The Mother. How shall I endure those orphaned days, knowing you to be in such a place?

The Daughter. Do not grieve overmuch for that. To you indeed the place seems very dark and terrible. So at first it seemed to me also, till I grew familiar with it at last ; and then it seemed not so terrible as pitiful.

The Mother. If the gods turned pitiful, they would die.

The Daughter. Yes.

The Mother. We are gods of the living, not of the dead.

The Daughter. Yet the dead have their god.

The Mother. Cursed for evermore! O child, what shall be said of him, whom all the other gods abhor— but we most of all?

The Daughter. I do not hate him.

The Mother (*astonished beyond measure*).   What? . . . (*In a changed tone*) You love him?

The Daughter.   Neither do I love him.

The Mother.   Why will you talk in riddles?

The Daughter.   He has his task, as the gods of heaven and of earth have theirs.   Their life is full of laughter and music, but on his face a smile never comes.   He took me from the glad upper air, and forced me down to his world of sad colours and faint sounds and bloodless forms.   That was hard to forgive.

The Mother.   It is not to be forgiven.

The Daughter.   When I came there the dead welcomed me, as the storm-driven sailor welcomes the unclouding of the stars.   My sorrow was their blessing.

The Mother.   Their blessedness was too dearly purchased.

The Daughter.   No, for I came to find my blessedness in theirs.

The Mother.   What?   In so passionless a thing?

The Daughter.   The living have their gift of life. The dead have nothing but our care to comfort them.— Mother, I have learned a strange new wisdom!   Immortality belongs to the feebler gods, and man in his heart honours none but those who die for him.

The Mother.   Strange wisdom indeed!

The Daughter.   Because I have made my dwelling under the earth, men will love me more than all the happy gods. . . . Also I am queen of the famous nations of the dead, who are more in number than all the living.

The Mother.   To know your greatness there is little consolation to me here.

The Daughter.   My place is not more there than here.

The Mother. But this cruel alternation! Every year to find and lose you again, and this, year after year, for ever!

The Daughter. It is the law of life. Night follows day, and day night; the flowers wither and grow again in the spring; in the spring the serpent renews his freshness and his youth. We too, if we are to share the life of earth, must die and be born again like the corn and the poppy in the corn. . . O mother, do not grieve for that! Let the high gods content themselves with nectar and the dance. We shall know a joy more divine because it is born of sorrow. We shall live in the heart of man through all their changing dynasties. For when they fall, they fall for ever; but our honour will never fail among men, because we share their sorrow and their joys.

The Mother. O mothers till the end of time, all your joys and sorrows have descended upon me.

The Daughter. We will bear the burden together. —Lean on me, mother, for now I am the stronger. . . . Let us go now. The sun has risen, and the earth is alive and glad.

> *They go out.*
> *After an interval the Man and the Girl are heard outside talking excitedly.*

The Man. Did you see that?

The Girl. What?

The Man. A great snake. I never saw so huge a snake, nor one that glittered so. It came out of the house. It slipped into these bushes.

The Girl. Will you follow it?

The Man. No. . . . It had a strange look—so

huge and shining !   It looked like a holy beast.   It had a beard.

> *They enter the house in some trepidation.   Their garments are draggled with the wet.   The Girl is carrying a basket full of weeds.*

The Man.   Nothing here. . . . How are the vines ?

The Girl.   O father, it is a miracle !   The vines have turned red with the young buds in a night.   And the olives and figs are sprouting too.

The Man.   The wheat is showing a finger's breadth above the ground already.   And I heard a landrail among the fennel in the valley.

The Girl.   I wonder what became of the old woman.

The Man.   Who knows but she may have been a mighty god, who ate at our table ?

The Girl.   At any rate she brought us luck.

ALCESTIS AND HER HERO

THE *Alcestis* of Euripides has certain peculiarities of
the kind that attract discussion. For example, it has
the structure and special diction of the Greek Tragedy ;
and in spirit also much of it is purely tragic. Yet—
quite against the ancient rule and almost definition of a
tragedy—it ends happily; while there are scenes in it
which come near to be farcical. Is it then a tragedy or
a comedy? Or is it neither, is it a satyr-play? These
questions have vexed and divided scholars. The
answer is that the *Alcestis* is none of these things ; it is
something new. The old scholar who wrote an *Argument* of our play says as much. The *Alcestis* is 'rather
of the satyric order '—not a satyr-drama, but something
like it. We ascertain further that it came last in the
series of four plays, the *tetralogy*, to which it belonged.
Now, normally, the fourth play was satyric. The
scholiast is clearly right : the *Alcestis* is not a satyr-
drama but something like it. Professor Murray, who
has been left to state the obvious facts of the case,
suggests the term ' pro-satyric '.

It is as simple as that. Not that I would pay the
reader with words ; my very purpose being to meet
the difficulty I fancy forming itself in his mind. I
realize that ' pro-satyric ' may affect him much as the
scientific names you see on little slips of wood in

botanic gardens affect the man who has no botany ; he disregards the Latin and looks at the flowers. The reader may say : 'Your *satyric* and *pro-satyric* are mere labels. To me they convey no meaning at all. And what do I lose? Take Shakespeare : I do not know what to call *The Tempest* or *As You Like It*, but my ignorance does not in the least interfere with my enjoyment of them. So you may give the *Alcestis* any of the titles in Polonius' list of possible varieties of drama. It does not matter.'

It does matter.

This question involves one of those profound and fundamental differences between ancient and modern literature on which I have been perhaps wearisomely insisting. The whole character of a Greek play is determined by its classification. If it is a tragedy, if it is a comedy, if it is a satyr-play—in each case it must rigorously obey a different complex of traditional conventions. Modern literature has something analogous in its rondeaus and ballades and such things. If you write a ballade you must observe the rules of the game. If you break even the least of them, your poem may be very charming, but it will not be a ballade. So a Greek tragedy or comedy or satyric play had to be written according to its definite prescription. Now suppose we put the problem of the *Alcestis* in this way : 'Did Euripides attempt to write a satyr-play and fail ? Or did he invent for himself a new form of drama ?' You see it does make a difference.

But there is more in it. In modern literature the spirit creates its appropriate form ; in ancient literature the form is given and must be filled by its appropriate spirit. Now formally the *Alcestis* is a tragedy, or at least (to put ourselves on quite safe ground) much closer to a tragedy than a comedy.   Let us restate the problem in these terms: 'Did Euripides intend or did he not intend *Alcestis* for a tragedy?'   If he did he has not filled the whole, but only a part of it, with the genuine tragic spirit; and there are whole scenes, like the altercation between Admetus and his father, which can only be explained if we suppose with Sir Richard Jebb that Euripides was devoid of any faintest sense of humour. But if Euripides did not mean the scene to be tragic at all—would that not make a difference?   Of course it would; it makes all the difference between good art and bad.

To understand what 'pro-satyric' might mean, we must know the meaning of 'satyric'.   It is not very easy to know, for the evidence bearing on the satyr-play is really very slight, and some of it variously interpreted. There is one entire example: the *Cyclops* of Euripides. There have been discovered recently considerable fragments of the *Ichneutai* or *Trackers* of Sophocles. Beyond that our first hand evidence scarcely goes.   We infer from it that in the time of Sophocles and Euripides the satyr-drama was of course comic, that it regularly had a chorus of satyrs, and that it was written—this is very surprising—in the set tragic diction.   A very curious form, obviously, and (you would suppose) not a promising one.   Nor do I think that very much can be said for the *Cyclops*.   It is quite amusing if you do not go to it expecting something like the *Birds* or the *Frogs*, but accept it on its own terms, which are not those of a comedy at all, but rather of a burlesque of tragedy. But if the *Cyclops* is a typical satyr-play, it is certain that the *Alcestis* is none.   It does not have the chorus

9

of satyrs. The language almost never actually condescends—and never very far—but keeps its grace and dignity even in describing the feasting of Heracles. The *Alcestis* seems to be a new type of play, the invention—and a delightful and beautiful one—of Euripides himself. We are told that the subject had been treated before; and the power of tradition was so great upon the Greek stage that we may assume that Euripides had before him the model of Phrynichus' *Alcestis* (and perhaps of a number of plays on the same matter which have not been recorded) when he composed his own drama. The *Alcestis* of Phrynichus does not survive. If it did, we should be able to decide how far it influenced our *Alcestis*. The probability is that the play of the older dramatist was pure satyric. The reasons for thinking this will appear; they are reasons of tradition.

The story of Alcestis was itself traditional. We have seen that it was put on the stage long before Euripides; Phrynichus was writing before the Persian Wars. Phrynichus may have taken it either from some earlier poet or from the great mass of unwritten legend. The story is told in the *Bibliotheca* of mythology attributed to the scholar Apollodorus:

' When Admetus was king of Pherae, Apollo became his serf. Admetus was seeking to wife Alcestis the daughter of Pelias. When Pelias proclaimed that he would give his daughter in marriage to the man who should yoke lions and wild boars in a chariot, Apollo yoked them and gave them to Admetus, who brought them to Pelias; and so obtains Alcestis. But when he was sacrificing at his marriage he forgot to sacrifice to Artemis. Therefore, when he opened the marriage

chamber, he found it full of coilin serpents. But
Apollo, bidding him appease the goddess, made request
of the Fates that, when Admetus was bound to die, he
might be released from death, if someone freely consented to die for him.   When the day came for his
dying, Alcestis died in his stead, since both his father
and his mother refused. And Persephone sent her back
to upper air again, or (as some say) Heracles saved her
after fighting with Hades.'

To read 'Apollodorus' is to wander in the Valley of
Dry Bones. But he is useful to the student of mythology
because he invents nothing and because he could draw
from sources now sealed to us.   In the case of this
story of Alcestis the mythologist has an additional
security ; it is essentially identical with a hundred other
stories he knows.   They are all ritual stories or myths.
The ritual which they express represents the death and
resurrection of some sacred being.   There must have
been, to account for her myth, a ceremony in which the
Passing and the Return of Alcestis were enacted. That
form of rite was to be found everywhere in ancient
Greece, as we know both from the written evidence and
from the remains of Greek art, which frequently represent the resurrection of a Divine Woman literally being
dug or hacked out of the ground by creatures inscribed
'Satyrs'. Her worshippers might call her here Korê,
and Semelê there, and Alcestis somewhere else.   At
heart, under all these names, and in spite of local
variations in her ritual, the *Rediviva* is everywhere one
and the same, being in fact the Earth, who appears to
die in winter and come to life again in the spring.   In
her resurrection aspect she was most widely known as
Korê, 'the Maiden', the young Earth (at least that

is how we explain her; her actual worshippers very properly would not rationalize her) married to Pluto or Hades, the god of the underworld and the dead. The *Bibliotheca*, you remember, says that according to one account Alcestis was restored to life by Persephone. Persephone is the more familiar name of the goddess also named Korê. The Greek in fact says Korê here.

The Chorus, addressing Alcestis in Euripides' play, says :

> *Minstrels many shall praise thy name*
> > *With lyre full-strung and with voices lyreless,*
> *When Mid-Moon riseth, an orbèd flame,*
> > *And from dusk to dawning the dance is tireless;*
> > *And Carnos cometh to Sparta's call,*
> > *And Athens shineth in festival;*
> *For thy death is a song, and a fullness of fame,*
> > *Till the heart of the singer is left desireless.*

This is to say, at the solemn feast of the *Carnea* at Sparta, and on some similar occasion at Athens, the legend of Alcestis was chanted, and probably in some way dramatically rendered. But Athens and Sparta are not Pherae ; and Pherae (one is almost bound to suppose) must be the true home of her myth and of the rite with which the myth was associated. Was the story of Alcestis annually represented in song and action at Pherae? It looks as if it was. She had a known and conspicuous tomb there.

HERACLES.
Where lies the tomb?—Where shall I find her now?

SERVANT.
Close by the straight Larissa road. The tall
White marble showeth from the castle wall.

That it existed in Euripides' time, and was regarded as a holy monument, is implied in the following words of the Chorus :

> *Let not the earth that lies upon her*
> *Be deemed a grave-mound of the dead.*
> *Let honour, as the Gods have honour,*
> *Be hers, till men shall bow the head,*
> *And strangers, climbing from the city*
> *Her slanting path, shall muse and say :*
> *" This woman died to save her lover,*
> *And liveth blest, the stars above her :*
> *Hail, Holy One, and grant thy pity !"*
> *So pass the wondering words away.*

νῦν δ᾽ἐστι μάκαιρα δαίμων—'Now is she a blessed Spirit' or Daemon ; surely that is clear enough. She must have been worshipped at Pherae. That her cult was connected with the great prehistoric tomb on the road to Larissa is certain both from the nature of her legend (a death and resurrection myth) and from what Euripides says. Now from what we know of ceremonies held throughout Greece in honour of dead 'Heroes' we may conjecture that athletic games were periodically celebrated in memory of Alcestis. If they were, it might explain a somewhat curious speech of Heracles in the play. When he comes back from the tomb with the veiled Alcestis, he pretends at first that she is a prize won by him at a wrestling, which has just been held somewhere near. These games, as Verrall saw, must have been in honour of Alcestis. And if this detail was not invented by Euripides, but was a part of the tradition as he received it, the games must have been traditional too. But it is a little matter, and there is no proof.

There are many undesigned correspondences which reveal the authenticity of the Alcestis myth. Korê was married to Pluto, 'the Wealthy', lord of the dead: Alcestis was married to Admetus lord of Pherae in Thessaly. *Admetus*, 'the Unsubdued', is one of the many names given to the god also called Pluto. Again, the wealth of Admetus was proverbial. He was especially rich in cattle. Naturally so, for in primitive times a man's wealth is mainly reckoned by the number of his cows. Now we find 'the cows of Admetus' mentioned in terms which imply that they were identical with the cows of Hades—who is Pluto. Again, the hospitality of Admetus was proverbial; and the Hospitable—'He of the Many Guests'—is one of the surnames bestowed (without any original irony) on the god of the dead. The parallel will look less fanciful when we have penetrated deeper into the story.

One fixed element in the tradition (so far as it pertains to Admetus) is the sojourn with him of the god Apollo in guise of a herdsman. Apollo, to avenge the death of his son Asclepius, slew the Cyclôpes. Whereupon Zeus ordained that Apollo should pass a year in thraldom to a mortal. 'And he came to Pheres' son Admetus in Pherae, and was a shepherd in his service, and caused all his cows to bear twins.' That is the reduced prose of the *Bibliotheca*. The poetry is to be found in many places from the choral odes in the *Alcestis* to *Phoebus with Admetus*. So beautiful and famous a legend is explained by scholars as originating in this way: it mythically expresses the temporary obscuration of the Light-god or Sun-god, although of course, poetically, it expresses exactly

as much as you are able to find in it. The early
Greeks, watching the daily disappearance of the sun
under the western horizon and his reappearance in the
east, explained this to themselves by supposing that he
passed through the underworld by night, shining to the
dead. In the paradise of Pindar the dead have their
sun and moon. The Sun, in Homer, threatens that, if
he is not avenged upon the Companions of Odysseus,
he will pass down into the house of Hades and shine
among the dead. Hence (by a kind of paradox very
strange to us but a commonplace of ancient religion)
the Sun-god comes to be identified with the god of the
dead. Helios is only the bright side of Hades. Now,
the oxen of the Sun recur constantly in mythology;
and they turn out to be really the same as the oxen of
Hades or Admetus. That is why it is so natural for
Apollo to keep the herds of Admetus. In one (only
in one) aspect of his nature he *is* Admetus. The lions
and the wild boars drawing the bridal car which brings
Alcestis to her new home from Iolcus are the familiar
beasts of Apollo, the same that gathered to his harping.

It was to Admetus in his shining aspect—as it were
the Sun-god himself—that Alcestis was married on the
day of that strange procession. In his other aspect she
is the bride of Death. Both Admetus and Alcestis have
this double nature like all these primitive nature spirits,
who die to live again. But another belief has helped to
mould her legend. The Greeks loved to represent the
death of a maiden as her marriage to the god of the
dead. And so Alcestis marrying Admetus is Alcestis
dying. The mythopoeic imagination plays endless
variations on a single theme. According to one variant
of the myth (known to Euripides, as some words

assigned to Heracles imply) it was Korê who restored Alcestis to the sunlight. And the Chorus pray that their queen may be *throned by the side of Hades' Bride*, that is Persephone or Korê. The Greek word—παρεδρεύοις—expresses a position of almost equal authority. And that is quite in order.

The other version of the myth said that Heracles wrestled with Death and forced Alcestis from his grasp. This is the version adopted by Euripides. It has certain obvious dramatic advantages over the other ; but is it equally authentic? Has Heracles, as the most famous of Greek heroes, been brought into an older story and confused its original form? It looks probable enough, indeed it may be regarded as certain ; for Heracles has no original connexion with Pherae, he comes from farther south. But he has not been thrust into the Alcestis legend without other recommendation than his popularity. He has taken the place (we must suppose) of some local Hero ; taken it in virtue of a radical affinity which made identification easy.

But besides all this Alcestis has a special claim upon Heracles.

One of the most characteristic institutions of Greek life was the *Kômos* or Revelling Procession. It was so ancient, so twisted about the roots of Greek society, that it had become as complex and elusive as life itself. We know not whether to call it a religious or (in the restricted sense) a social custom ; it was both. Nor can we justly call it either a dance or a procession or a choir or a revel-rout ; it was all these things at once. As for the members of the Kômos, they usually carried torches—this for a religious reason. They often dressed up as animals—again no doubt for some religious or magical reason. They had naturally a leader to head the procession, to guide the steps and gestures of the dance, to strike up the Kômos-song. This song was regularly of a festive or even a fescennine nature. A typical variety of it was the Marriage Song or *Hymenaeus*. Since this became a literary form, some exercises in which survive to us, we can guess at its original character from these, as: Catullus' poem on the marriage of Torquatus. It may remind us that the marriage procession was perhaps the most complete and representative form of the Kômos. The bride and bridegroom, amid flowers and music, were conducted in a chariot to his house. The evidence indicates that the bridegroom was regarded as in some sense a Victor or even a King, like the Beloved in the *Song of Solomon*. Conversely, the celebration of a victory was apt to take the form of a marriage of the victor ; as at Olympia the victor in the Games, triumphing at the head of his Kômos, was regarded as the bridegroom of the winner in the women's race.

The confusion of thought seems complete. It is not really so ; but, although there is a clue, it must be admitted that it cannot be unwound to the end. It is impossible to frame a set of words which shall not be at once too narrow and too wide to cover the emotions which created the Kômos ; too narrow because they will confine those emotions to a single form of their expression, too wide in respect that this form will be of a definiteness that the sentiment of the Kômos never attained. The sentiment is like a cloud ; capable of any shape and fixable in none. If one *must* try for a word to suggest it, the best I think is *Niké*, which we translate Victory, but which means a great deal more than that. It was felt to bring increase of the power and numbers and wealth of the whole community to which the victor belonged, to bring luck, prestige, general 'victoriousness' as I must lamely express it, to the state. Or we may say: it was something more than a personal distinction, or even a distinction reflected upon the community through one of its number; it was also a powerful charm. The whole end and purpose of a Kômos was simply to work this charm. It was a piece of magic. The people sought to make itself victorious by behaving as if it were. Nowadays the newspapers do this for us.

The Kômos ceremony evolved its hero, its typical legendary Victor, much as Father Christmas, for example, is the projection of our Christmas customs. The function of Kômos-leader, successively filled by an endless line of human functionaries stretching into the remotest past, begat the concept of an ideal functionary, relegated by hard facts to the misty time of the Heroic Age. This typical Victor is Heracles.

Everything about him can be explained on this view of his nature. He is the embodiment of Nikê, his constant epithet *Kallinikos* 'winner of fair victory'. Therefore tradition makes him the founder of the great Olympic Games and the first Olympic victor. At every celebration of the Games the victor of the occasion led the Kômos of his triumphant followers to the altar of Zeus, singing the hymn composed, it was said, by Archilochus:

> *O Victor, hail, lord Heracles!*
> *Thyself and Iolaus, spearmen twain.*

The victor in fact personated Heracles. Nothing

helps us more to realize how much the conception of Heracles as the typical victor leading his rejoicing train dominated all others in the ancient mind than just this circumstance, that any human Kômos-leader at once suggested him. It was so in Greece, as the instance from Olympia and other instances show. It was so also at Rome, where the statue of Hercules *Victor* was dressed in triumphal robes whenever a general celebrated a triumph, which was essentially a Kômos.

Having remarked that the notion of victory was incomplete in the Greek mind without the thought of its celebration—as if a victory must be proclaimed before its full virtue could be extracted—what can we make of the apparent anomaly that it is not the Triumph of Heracles but his Labours that are the great theme of the literature concerned with him? It is explained when you reflect that literature could not help itself. The Triumph was a unique event; it was final, the conclusion. It was only the adventures that could be extended and developed in all directions. The arts that do not labour under this disability so much give in their predilection for the scene of the Triumph the right measure of its importance. We see Heracles entering Olympus in a triumphal car, renewed in youth and followed by a dancing and singing train of nymphs or satyrs or even gods. Nikê is a constant companion; sometimes he carries symbolically a little figure of her in his hand. He is also *Musagetes*, 'Leader of the Muses'; and the Muses, as you may discover in the *Theogony* of Hesiod, are a singing and dancing company. The traveller Pausanias found a representation of *Heracles accompanied by the Muses* at

Messana and at Sparta.   The Roman general Fuluius Nobilior set up a statue of *Hercules Musarum* 'because', Eumenius says, 'when he was commanding in Greece, he had heard that Heracles was *Musagetes*, that is, the Companion and Leader of the Muses'.

It is because Heracles was the projection of the Kômos, embodying and concentrating its qualities, that many *thiasi* or clubs at Athens were named after him ; for a *thiasus* might be called a Kômos in permanence. It is because he comes of the Kômos that he possesses unmeasured strength, that he is such an enormous eater and drinker, that he has so many children, that he is (in the true and original sense) *comic*.   He is all that the revellers desire their leader to be.

In an essay one can only touch on some of these points.   But they are vital.

There is, for instance, what one might call the marriage motive.   The ancient Kômos was apt to take the form of a marriage-pomp in which the Leader played the part of Bridegroom.   There was a ritual wedding (γάμος), which was of course a fertility charm. This aspect of the Kômos is reflected in the marriage of Heracles to Hebe, an essential part of his Triumph. There is evidence which makes it very probable that Heracles was worshipped in places as actually himself a marriage-god.   It was customary to write over the door of a newly married man :

The Son of Zeus, Heracles the Victor, dwells here.   Let nothing evil enter !

With the ancient marriage, and indeed probably with every Kômos, there went a certain amount of indecent badinage.   Hence the 'satyric' Heracles—the hero of so many satyr-plays.   But the ribaldry of the Kômos has a double motive. It is incentive, but it is also apotropaic. The real intention of the insulting *carmina* in the Roman triumph (for instance) was to avert the evil which threatens the overproud. The *triumphator* might deem himself a god and provoke the jealousy of Olympus, unless he were effectively reminded of his human case. So in the service of Heracles we find the practice of ritual cursing. The myth or explanation of the rite is to be found in the *Bibliotheca*.

'When he was traversing Asia he landed at Thermydrae, a harbour of the Lindians. There he loosed from the wain one of the steers of an ox-driver, and sacrificed it, and feasted. And the driver, unable to help himself, stood upon a hill and cursed him. Wherefore to this day, when they sacrifice to Heracles, they do it with curses'.

Heracles ate the whole ox at a sitting. The ritual abuse and cursing are thus brought into connexion with the *gluttony* of the hero. The leader of a Kômos was expected to eat and drink a great deal, that it might be a charm for the multiplying of food and wine. So Heracles was credited with a prodigious appetite—the subject of infinite jests. Even more expressive perhaps are the seriously bestowed cult-titles *Adêphagos*, 'Glutton', *Epitrapezios*, 'Who-sits-at-table'. There was at Athens an association or charity of 'Parasites', that is table-companions, of Heracles, who were maintained at the public expense. Many stories were told of his entertainment by mortals, as in our fable he is entertained by Admetus. Extraordinarily frequent in art is this subject of the *Feasting Heracles*. Alone, or in company, he reclines with a great goblet in his hand.

What economists call the 'food supply' is the first need of a primitive, or indeed of any, community. But the insuring of an abundance of things to eat is only one part of the business incumbent on Heracles as representative of the Kômos. He produces all the things the Kômos dances for. He causes gardens to blossom and fertilizing springs to burst forth. His club was not originally a weapon, but a branch of blossoming wild olive, the wild olive whose leaves formed the victor's crown at Olympia. Such a branch was an emblem or magical instrument of fertility, capable also of scaring away spirits of blight and evil. Sometimes Heracles is represented wearing a garland of the white poplar, or holding in his hand a twig or a flower or an apple ; very often with a cornucopia, which was a great horn brimmed with fruits. All these things were symbols of fruitfulness. Most significant perhaps of all, he was often carved in *herm* form, like the ithyphallic images of Hermes. Eros and he were frequently associated in worship. He was also reckoned one of the 'Idaean Dactyls', the 'eldest' of the Dactyls in fact ; whose special function was the magical induction of fertility by a dance or procession which might fairly be called a Kômos.

It is a curious but (on reflection) quite natural consequence of the victor's position as leader of the Kômos that he often personated, or was thought to represent the Sun, the father of magic and the evident fountain of light and life, and symbol of the victorious Summer. Thus at Olympia the victors in the men's and women's contests are thought to have personated, he the Sun, and she the Moon. The chariot of the victor or *triumphator* was drawn (when the ritual was perfect) by four horses, preferably white—the chariot and horses of the Sun. There is much to show that Heracles on one side of his nature came very near to Helios and Apollo. A great mass of his mythology has its roots in sun-worship. To deal with it here would involve too long an analysis; let me mention only the herds of Geryon and of Augeas, and the Cretan Bull—all cattle of the Sun. The meaning to the mythologist of these stories is that Heracles was, in the context they form, himself the Sun. He is the Sun when (according to another story) he sails across Oceanus in the golden cup of Helios. Like Helios, too, he is 'unwearied' and full of labours.

> ' Surely the Sun hath labour all his days,
> And never any respite, steeds nor god,
> Since Eos first, whose hands are rosy rays,
> Ocean forsook, and Heaven's high pathway trod;
> All night across the sea that wondrous bed
> Shell-hollow, beaten by Hephaistos' hand,
> Of wingèd gold and gorgeous, bears his head
> Half-waking on the wave from eve's red strand
> To the Ethiop shore, where steeds and chariot are,
> Keen hearted, waiting for the morning star.'

This aspect of Heracles affords us once more the opportunity of observing the curious and baffling, yet constantly repeated, phenomenon of the nature-religions. The characters of the myth dissolve and melt into one another, interchanging all but their names; for they are really one character viewed from different points or in different relations. Apollo, Admetus, Heracles are varying names for one divine being, a Power of light and life. And since in primitive religions the Power of light and life is at the same time the Power of darkness and death, Thanatos or Death, who seems in the play the enemy of all three, is in reality their double. Heracles fighting with Death in Pherae is like Heracles fighting with Hades at Pylos, like Heracles descending into the realm of Persephone. He received the cornucopia he often carries from Pluto, and the painters of vases are very fond of showing him in the underworld. He was worshipped along with Demeter and Korê—Korê with whom Alcestis is to be identified. But let us get this quite clear: when I say that Apollo, Admetus, and Heracles are at bottom identical, I mean in the Alcestis myth. Outside that context each developed new and comparatively alien phases of his nature. The phase they have in common happens to be particularly important for this legend; that is all. Or it may be put in this way: the legend has been created by their touching at a single point; and this touching was the result of a native affinity.

One other aspect of Heracles deeply concerns the *Alcestis*. The Kômos had a rite or traditional manner of behaviour, such as the Greeks called a *Drômenon*. It was some kind of mimetic representation of the victory which the Kômos was celebrating. It has been recognized quite recently what this *Drômenon* really is. It is closely similar, it must indeed be the same as the Folk Play, of which many versions have been preserved, and which in a more or less degenerate form is still acted in certain of the less accessible parts of Europe. The essence of it is a combat between the Hero and an Enemy, and the ultimate marriage of the Hero to his Bride. The Enemy may be human, or he may take the form of some monster. Sometimes the Hero kills his antagonist, sometimes he is himself killed. In the latter case, after his death has been duly lamented by the Bride, appears a magician or doctor, who restores the Hero to life. Follows the consummation of the marriage.

Heracles is the leader of the Kômos, and therefore the Hero of the *Drômenon.* How much of his mythology is illustrated if we see that! All the Labours have this in common: the Hero disappears on some generally distant and always perilous adventure, and then suddenly reappears triumphant. A certain Istros of Alexandria wrote a book on these 'Epiphanies of Heracles'. Where a god or an immortal is in question, such disappearance and reappearance are mythologically equivalent to death and resurrection. A god cannot be supposed truly to die, even temporarily. He can only be exiled, like Apollo to the house of Admetus; or descend into Hades like Dionysus. Ultimately, there being no more labours for him to accomplish, Heracles does die; but only apparently. Zeus casts a thunderbolt on Oeta, the pyre is quenched, and Heracles enters Olympus in triumph.

The Hero or 'Agonist' of the Folk Play is a pretty constant character; the 'Antagonist' takes many forms. In the class of Plays of which 'S. George and the Dragon' is the type the enemy is a dragon or a serpent or the like. To this class then belong the stories of Heracles strangling the serpents of Hera in his cradle, slaying the Hydra of Lerna, destroying the sea-monster in the Hesione-legend, smiting the snake of the Hesperides. The Antagonist is a lion in the stories of the Lion of Cithaeron and the Lion of Nemea. Often he is a bull—a formidable animal in antiquity, roaming half-wild over the unenclosed pastures. One of the Labours was the carrying off of the Cretan Bull. This

Bull, who is 'sacred to the Sun', reappears in the herds of Augeas and in the herds of Geryon.

Or the Antagonist may be human or semi-human: a Giant or an 'Arab' or a Wild Man or the like. Well, Heracles fights with the Centaurs of Pelion and those of Pholoe. He is constantly engaged in putting down local tyrants, *hubristai*. One is mentioned, rather more than incidentally, in the *Alcestis* : Diomedes of Thrace. The story of Diomedes' fire-breathing, man-devouring horses reflects a ritual in the savage old Thracian religion ; and in the other stories we should doubtless find in every case a native ritual accounting for the local legend, although it would be no longer possible in every case to reconstruct the ritual with any certainty. But observe that the myths, with whatever variety of detail, have all one plot: the Combat or *Agôn* with the Antagonist and the Victory of Heracles.—The Antagonist is a giant in the legends of Antaios, of Geryon, of Cacus, of Eurytion, of Eryx ; in the *Alcestis* Death. So also at Pylus Heracles wounds Hades. He smites also *Old Age, Epiales* or Fever, a *Kêr* or demon imp— stories best explained as growing out of mimetic cere- monies comparable to the 'Carrying out of Death' and similar customs described in the *Golden Bough*. Heracles with his leafy branch is leader of the Kômos which drives out Death and Winter.

Comedy is 'the song of the Kômos', Heracles its leader ; therefore Heracles is comic, *originally* comic, in this sense of the word. His history is pretty much the history of the Kômos itself. The comedy of literature, Aristotle tells us, had its source in the phallic songs sung by the Kômos under its leader or precentor ; such a song as we find in the *Acharnians* of Aristophanes addressed to the god Phales, and accompanied by some kind of *Drômenon* or dramatic ritual, which it is possible partly to make out in the brief scene of the *Acharnians* where it occurs. Tragedy, again, developed ἐκ τοῦ σατυρικοῦ, from a satyric original; and the diction of Sophoclean tragedy was 'elevated into seriousness' from its earlier ludicrous tone. If we let ourselves be convinced by these plain statements of Aristotle, we must conclude that the original forms of Greek comedy and tragedy (which, to begin with, was as much as comedy a choral performance) were singularly alike. Perhaps they were the same. Perhaps this original form survived under modification in the satyr-play. Recent investigation seems to points to that. Thus much is certain, tragedy underwent a long process of refinement and expurgation. Heracles shared in that development; the 'tragic' Heracles is later than the satyric. For although the Agôn which precedes the Victory, the death which precedes the Resurrection of the Hero, hold the germs of tragedy, in Heracles' case the insistence was at first chiefly on the Victory and the Resurrection, joyous events to be celebrated in the antique manner.

It is not then surprising to find that many of the Heracles legends are comic. They are not late stories nor the inventions of poets. A whole series deals with Heracles' feats of eating and drinking; tales born of the Kômos-feast and as old as the hero himself. One remembers too the Battle with the Pygmies, as ancient at least as Epicharmus; the adventure with the Cercôpes, a very old story; the legend of Omphale, reflecting a primitive rite of the Saturnalian class involving an exchange of clothes between the sexes.

We learn from Aristophanes that the Glutton Heracles was a stock character in the popular or 'vulgar' or 'Megarian' comedy. Epicharmus introduced him time and again into his plays, notably *The Marriage of Hebe*. Of the Attic writers of comedy, Cratinus wrote a *Busiris*, in which Heracles on the point of being immolated in Egypt suddenly rends his bonds and slays his would-be sacrificers; Pherecrates a *Pseudo-Heracles*; Hermippus a *Cercôpes*, in which however it is not absolutely certain that Heracles appeared; Archippus a *Heracles Marrying*. As for the satyr-play, it was long ago pointed out that Heracles belonged to it in quite a special way. He was particularly at home among satyrs, art constantly representing him in their company, and literature making him the chief hero of the satyr-play, as may be gathered from the *Fragments* of the tragic poets. On the other hand the tragic Heracles is comparatively late. He appeared at the end of the *Prometheus Unbound* of Aeschylus, where his business was to release Prometheus from his rock; and he appears at the end of Sophocles' *Philoctêtes*. Both episodes are in the nature of Epiphanies, bringing a happy conclusion to a painful story. He is not a truly tragic character in *Alcestis*. It was not indeed till he wrote the *Heracles* that Euripides was ready to break finally with the satyric tradition and make Heracles the subject of a tragedy. The example was followed in the *Women of Trachis*. So far as our information goes, Heracles was the hero of only two, and these not early, tragedies.

His treatment in the epos is very curious. Homer barely mentions him—does not mention him at all, some scholars would say, who believe the passages where his name occurs to be interpolations.   The reason seems clear: Heracles was still a somewhat grotesque figure of popular mythology with associations not at all consonant with the epic convention.   True, the Madness of Heracles was touched upon in the *Cypria*; and he must have come into the *Taking of Oichalia* and the *Aegimius*; while we possess the *Shield of Heracles*, where the treatment is heavily serious.   But how are we to date any part of these traditional poems? It is somewhat different with the *Heracleia*.   We can date Panyassis.   Before Panyassis, Pisander and a more shadowy Pisinous, both of Rhodes, worked at the poem.   It was in fact the traditional Rhodian epic. For some reason, which we may only conjecture, Heracles became the national hero of the Dorians. Naturally therefore in the Dorian island of Rhodes the tendency would arise to represent him worthily and epically.   It could be done by working in the spirit which has cleansed the Homeric Poems of all the gross and ugly and silly things in the old saga-material. Thereby, however, the traditional conception of Heracles was not one whit affected.   And it is this conception which finds expression in the Drama, because the Drama holds closer than the Epic to the fixed *Drômenon* with its Kômos.   And so the comic Heracles is not epic burlesque, although of course, after he became a figure of the heroic saga, a piquancy was added to the fun by travesty of the epic hero.

It is Heracles who chiefly gives the *Alcestis* its satyric colour.   Euripides to be sure does not treat him in the mere spirit of farce; to regard the Heracles of *Alcestis* as purely farcical is to spoil the peculiar quality of its appeal.   One fails to understand how exquisite a piece of art it is, until one grasps the nature of the problem Euripides proposed to himself. Suppose he had written a satyr-play of the traditional sort; what would it have been like? If we had the *Alcestis* of Phrynichus, very likely the question would be answered for us. As it is, the satyric form has certain characteristics so marked; and the comic possibilities of the story are so clear; that we can be almost sure of the main lines a satyric *Alcestis* would follow.

To begin with: we must assume that there would be a Chorus of satyrs. Heracles is the natural centre and leader of their band; compare the position of Silenus in the *Cyclops*. Taking this as given, we may so far follow the order of events in Euripides as to suppose a Prologue in which Apollo and Death appear and abuse one another *more satyrico*. Death—a grotesque figure like a great black bird—accuses Apollo of making the Fates drunk and then taking advantage of their drunken complaisance to procure for Admetus a conditional respite from death. Following the Prologue, the Chorus would come in, perhaps with Heracles at their head, and sing their first *ode*. What next? One can hardly suppose that the death of Alcestis would be represented in a satyr-play. The death scene (it is worth observing) is really quite short in Euripides; and this is what we should expect if it was an innovation in the traditional plot, Greek art always reducing innovation to a minimum. But the altercation between Admetus and his father must surely belong to the old plot, and must come in; and so must the scene in which Heracles drunkenly moralizes on human destiny. The gloomy servant too, complaining to the audience of Heracles' manners at table, is conceived quite in the spirit of Greek comedy.   Ultimately Heracles, having learned the truth about Alcestis, sets out for her tomb to catch Death and squeeze the breath out of him till he surrenders his prey.   The finale is the triumphant reappearance of the hero with Alcestis and the celebration of his victory by the Kômos of satyrs. Normally in this scene Heracles and Alcestis should appear as (what in a sense they are) Bridegroom and Bride.   But perhaps even the satyric plot had come to accept the present ending, and Alcestis was restored to Admetus.

What Euripides does is to soften down the grotesque elements of the story until we just feel that they are there, lurking possibilities of laughter, giving a faintly ironic but extraordinarily human quality to the pathos of the central situation.   Death remains a somewhat *macabre* figure and slightly ridiculous; yet, if you laugh, it is, as we say, with the wrong side of your mouth.   Apollo's trick to beguile the Fates is no more than hinted at.   The quarrel between Admetus and Pheres is characteristically seized to throw a vivid and rather merciless light on the psychology of father and son.   The drunkenness of Heracles is a very mild affair.   The Triumph of the Hero resolves itself into a somewhat protracted and curious scene in which Heracles appears with Alcestis veiled—it seems worth remarking that a Greek bride wore a concealing veil— and pretends to Admetus that she is a prize won at some games in the neighbourhood.   I think the explanation may be that the scene was traditional, and originally comic; it is not without a humorous element even in Euripides, and one does not require much imagination to see the amount of comic 'business' which could be imported into it. The Kômos-procession, which in a satyr-play must have followed the reunion of husband and wife, has been quietly omitted. The satyrs have made way for a tragedy chorus of Elders.

But what makes the *Alcestis* so original is not a mere readjustment of emphasis; it is not even the treatment of a satyric subject in the form and spirit of Greek Tragedy, for this could have been no innovation (since only in this way could Tragedy progress at all); it is the unique commingling of two spirits. One is the characteristic Euripidean spirit, sad, disenchanted, subtle, rebellious, ironical, sympathetic, hungry for beauty, hungrier for justice. The other is the jovial, tolerant spirit of the satyric tradition. In all Euripides' work we observe the meeting of cross-currents. Nowhere out of the *Alcestis* do we find this undercurrent of a satirical humour; and nowhere else do the various streams flow together so quietly and, as it were, so naturally. It is perhaps the most human of all his dramas, though not the greatest. The characters approach more nearly the level of ordinary humanity. We can not only accept them, we know them, we have lived with them. It was just that slight relaxation of the tragic tension in *Alcestis* which enabled Euripides to get this effect by permitting him to dwell a little on the minor human weaknesses which are the proper subject of Comedy. It might indeed be argued without too much paradox that the method of the *Alcestis* in some ways resembles the method of Modern Comedy (as, for example, Meredith practised it) more closely than anything in Aristophanes.

Every character in the play is intensely realized. Admetus has the artistic temperament. The farewell scene between Alcestis and him always reminds me of *Any Wife to Any Husband*:

> *I know that nature ! Pass a festive day,*
> *Thou dost not throw its relic-flower away*
> *Nor bid its music's loitering echo speed. . . .*

He is selfish in the way of a spoilt child or a spoilt artist. Impossible for him to exist without admiration. It is partly this need, one feels, which makes him yield hospitality to Heracles at a moment so trying for everybody. When the leader of the Chorus remonstrates, Admetus answers :

> *And had I turned the stranger from my door,*
> *Who sought my shelter, hadst thou praised me more ?*
> *I trow not, if my sorrow were thereby*
> *No whit less, only the more friendless I.*
> *And more, when bards tell tales, were it not worse*
> *My house should lie beneath the stranger's curse ?*

Heracles nor any one else would have 'cursed' him for closing his doors under the circumstances. But Admetus sees the opportunity for a shining display of 'magnanimity', sees himself in the poets—as it were in the newspapers. This, while Alcestis (who died for him) is being carried to her grave. Yet somehow one does not hate him ; perhaps because Alcestis loved him, perhaps because his need of admiration is not greater than his need of affection, perhaps because he is a commoner type than the stronger sex cares to admit. One even gets a little sorry for him after Pheres (that very vital old man) has stripped him of all his comfortable pretences—a bitter experience for our egoist. The fine speeches grow rarer and rarer; and at last cease altogether.

It is difficult to say anything at all about Alcestis, she is so whole and single. If she had not done what she did, the temptation would have been to call her characterless. She is very instinctive and feminine, with none of a man's desire to act up to a situation imposing the ideal test of the professedly masculine virtues. Think of Admetus in her place; what 'noble sentiments' we should have had! Never was a less stagey heroine. Considering that it is she who makes the play, it is astonishing how little she says; but her very inarticulateness expresses and endears her to us. She is conventional, practical, rooted in domesticities. One suspects that her children are more to her than her husband, although she loves him too in a protecting, maternal way. She is extraordinarily true to type, and her example shows of what the type is capable.

Heracles is a very attractive character. He is a big jovial man with a great deal of good sense and kindly feeling under that rough lion-skin of his. He is that at all times; but he is sometimes more. One of the finest things in the play is the revelation, at the call of an extreme danger, of the heroic strain in this unassuming son of the god. We are made to feel that the roystering mood of the feast was but the mask of a more permanent mood, a kind of cheerful stoicism, accepting, though fully conscious of, the burden of its duty. His few last words break a sort of supernatural light over his going, and we forget Alcestis for the moment as we watch the suffering, kindly hero fare onwards into the mists of the North to do battle with the Thracian savage.

Euripides has made us accept that transfiguration as natural, inevitable. This is great art. Yet it merely enforces the stroke of genius which created a new kind of drama, full of possibilities since realized, taking us into a region where laughter and tears and mockery and admiration familiarly mingle. We moderns have wandered much in that region, and so perhaps understand Euripides better here than the ancients themselves in general understood him. So vital a matter was it for their art to preserve the purity of the type, the continuity of the tradition. Whereas the *Alcestis* was an experiment.

Note

The translations from the " Alcestis" are taken from Gilbert Murray's version (London 1915), the translation of Mimnermus' fragment on Helios from the same scholar's History of Greek Literature.

A NOTE ON GREEK SIMPLICITY

We have been told so often that Greek art is studious of simplicity, that we have come to receive this with the kind of weary acceptance which we accord to the commonplaces of criticism. But what does it mean? There are all kinds of simplicity, from the naive to the ironical. Which is the characteristically Greek kind? I cannot remember that the question has ever been answered; although it specially deserves to be faced, because the answer is certainly not obvious. I fancy that the experience of most who have studied Greek art simply for the pleasure it can give is this :—You are struck at first by the simplicity and severity of outline. You may be a little chilled by it perhaps. Then, as you return—and Greek art lures you back as no other—you seem to yourself to discover a new significance every time, an enigmatic and secret something not on the surface. This is true of all art indeed, or at least of all great art; one is always finding fresh meanings in it. But it is not sufficiently recognized as true of Greek art. It is supposed that anybody with eyes in his head can appreciate it at a glance. But it is not true; the appeal of Greek art is a very subtle one. So to talk about Greek 'simplicity' may easily become misleading, if we think all has been said when we have remarked that the Greeks

were, compared with ourselves, a simple people. Were
they?

Simplicity is not an invariable element in Greek
style. Pindar is not a simple writer, nor is Aeschylus,
nor Thucydides. When one comes to think of it, it
must chiefly be Homer, with Herodotus and Xenophon
perhaps next in order of importance, who has made
us believe that the Greeks preferred to write simply.
In actual fact it all depended on considerations which
we are constantly disregarding, whether a man wrote
simply or not. We have got to disabuse our minds
of a great many preconceptions before we can even
begin the discussion of Greek simplicity in style. One
of the worst concerns this very word 'style'. Style as
the wreaking of the artist's personality upon whatever
matter he may select is not a Greek conception at all,
but a peculiarly modern one. To the Greek style was
a traditional way of writing ; not a way of writing of
your own, but the opposite. It is more accurate, however, to speak of styles than of style in Greek literature. The matter determined the manner. If you
chose an epic subject, you must treat it in the consecrated epic style. If you would write a choral lyric,
you must employ a wholly different metre, diction, and
poetic method. It belonged to a different genus or
Kind, and to confuse the Kinds was bad art. The epic
manner was simple and direct ; the choric ode tended
to be complex and ornate. Here is one, and only one,
of many large and important exceptions to be taken to
the statement that simplicity is a note of Greek literature. It is only broadly true.

What we need, then, is a definition of simplicity.
Failing that, we shall find it useful to make at least

certain distinctions. There is, to begin with, the simplicity of the man who has none but simple thoughts and simple words in which to express them. For example :—

And they heard the voice of the Lord walking in the garden in the cool of the day : and Adam and his wife hid themselves from the presence of the Lord God amongst the trees of the garden.

He maketh me to lie down in green pastures : he leadeth me beside the still waters.

> *In somer when the shawes be sheyne,*
> *And leaves be large and long,*
> *Hit is fully merry in feyre foreste*
> *To here the foulys song.*

This kind of simplicity is common enough in Greek literature. It could not be otherwise, for the Greeks were the first people who really mastered the art of self-expression, and they had to learn. They could only learn by sloughing one cortex after another of intellectual sloth and helplessness—*naiveté* and *niaiserie*. Herodotus calls the process 'getting rid of silly simplicity'. Greek literature might be regarded as the expression in words of this process ; for the most characteristic thing about the Greek mind is the effort it is always making to escape from silliness. Simplicity, even in the 'pure' form I have been illustrating, need not be 'silly'. The passages quoted are not so, even in the Greek sense. But they may perhaps be fairly called simple-minded. And I think the whole movement of Greek literature is away from simple-mindedness or 'silly simplicity' to another kind, which is almost its opposite—the studied simplicity of the artist.

One naturally begins with Homer. Simplicity is one of the four qualities which Matthew Arnold noted as characteristic of Homer. Arnold was much too sensitive in matters of style to be misled by a word into any fancy that Homer's simplicity was the effect of an immature or half-accomplished art, charming us by a kind of unstudied or accidental grace. There is no unstudied or accidental beauty in Homer, except what may be the gift of that fortune, which, as the Greek saying has it, often favours the artist. There is nothing Homer cannot say, no gorgeousness or subtlety he cannot reach, in that simple style of his, which is of all styles ever written the most perfect in its own kind, and the most adequate to its own purposes. I need not give more than two instances to show what I mean. If the reader disagrees with my commentary upon them, let him consider that this itself is a proof that the Homeric simplicity may hide something which is capable of more than one interpretation.

I take my first instance from the tenth Book of the *Iliad*, known in antiquity as *The Poetry about Dolon*. It relates the slaying of a Trojan spy by Odysseus and Diomede. We get a vivid impression of the spy—an ugly man, with the thin legs of the runner. He is interested in horses. He is boastful, conceited, and excessively, incredibly vain. Nothing less will serve than that he should ride in triumph in the captured chariot of Achilles, drawn by the divine horses. To appreciate the full audacity of this aspiration one has to remember that driving in a four-horse chariot was to the

average Greek the summit of human glory, so that
the man who did it was apt to feel himself a god and by
the multitude to be regarded as such.   And here the
car must be Achilles'!   To procure all this, Dolon
volunteers on a service of the deadliest danger.   He
realizes the peril intensely, for he is an imaginative man
—the sort of man who thinks it a fine idea to dress up as
a wolf and crawl on all fours through the darkness into
the enemy's camp.   His imagination makes him reck-
lessly brave one moment, and panic-stricken the next.
All this is indicated in far fewer words than I have used.
And then Homer quietly adds this line :

He was an only son among five sisters.

Could anything be simpler than that ?   Could anything
be more subtle ?

My second instance will be one which Arnold himself
selected.   Achilles, 'seeing red' in a frenzy of wrath
and grief for the death of Patroclus, overtakes and has
at his mercy Lycaon, a son of Priam.   Once before
Lycaon had fallen into the hands of Achilles, in earlier
days of the war, when mercy had not yet been quite
shut out from the hearts of the fighters.   He had been
caught at night in the king's garden cutting young
branches from a wild figtree 'to make handrails for
a chariot', and had been sold into slavery in the island
of Lemnos.   He had been ransomed at last, and reached
Troy, and for eleven days made merry in the company
of his friends, and on the twelfth day went forth to the
fighting.   And now here was Achilles again. . . . The
words in which the boy pleads vainly for his life are
extraordinarily distressing ; you want to put your hands

to your ears. (And yet it has been said that the *Iliad*
is a glorification of war.) ' Have pity upon me. . . .
Once before I tasted bread with thee, when thou madest
me captive in the orchard, and soldest me into Lemnos,
taking me from my father and my friends. . . . This is
the twelfth day since I came to Ilium after that suffering.
And now my cruel portion hath put me once again
beneath thy hand. . . . I think God must hate me, who
hath given me to thee a second time. . . . Life hath
not been granted me for long. My mother. . . .' He
makes all kinds of hopeless, irrelevant appeals, as he
crouches grasping the knees of Achilles with one hand,
and the terrible spear with the other. ' Our mother had
two of us, and thou wilt be the slaughterer of both.
Thou hast slain Polydorus . . . and now, here, it will
go hard with me. . . . Do not kill me ; Hector's
mother is not mine '—as if that perhaps would touch
some prejudice in favour of the mother, lingering on
from days when Aegean men may have reckoned
descent on the maternal side, or likely in any case to
exist in Achilles, to whom Thetis is so much more than
poor old Peleus.

' Hector ', pursues Lycaon, ' who slew thy comrade,
that was gentle and strong.' It was a fatal thing to say.
For it brings back, with a fresh vividness that hurts like
a sudden blow, the image of Patroclus to the mind of
the man who loved him. Achilles interrupts the suppliant with a terrible and marvellous outburst. I think
he had been touched a little by the youth and beauty
of the young Trojan prince, just as he was to be moved
later by the beauty and sorrow of Priam. But he was
not going to be unfaithful even in thought to his friend.
So he cries ' Die thou also ! Why dost thou so bemoan

thyself?   Patroclus is dead. . . .'   I have left untranslated a single word, one of the commonest in Greek, yet the very word which makes the line where it occurs one of the most wonderful in poetry.   It is φίλος—something a little less than 'beloved', but certainly, in the context, a great deal more than 'friend.'   'Nay, O φίλος, die thou also!'   There are commentators who think this is spoken ironically—I do not know whether from ignorance of human nature, or at least of Greek human nature; or because they are shocked; or because the poetry escapes them.   At any rate they make the passage horrible.

The simplicity of these lines is—one must be pardoned the paradox—a very complex matter.   There is no single word for a quality which lays hold on you from so many sides at once.   One can say what it is not ; it is not inarticulate.   We constantly feel in reading the Bible, and great areas of medieval literature, that the writers are just learning to write and would say more if they could.   We feel about the Greeks that they could say more if they would.   The suggestion of inarticulateness has a charm of its own—*loquela ipso offensantis linguae jragmine dulcior.*   Part of the attraction for us in the earlier poems of Morris and the marionette-plays of Maeterlinck lies in the way they have, by deliberate art of course, recaptured this very charm. But it is very rare indeed in Greek literature.   The *Suppliant Women* of Aeschylus has it, I think, here and there, where the struggle of the language to escape from the ritual formula into the free dramatic sentence is palpable enough, as you notice by contrast when you come to the choric odes, where the poet shows himself the untroubled master of the rarest and most magical lyric tones.   But it remains true that Greek literature makes all others, with the partial exception of French, look verbose and maladroit by comparison, and does this chiefly by means of a simplicity which is anything but inarticulate.

Achilles says to Priam

It is said, old man, that thou also wert happy once.

What array of words could say so much?   One has to go to the *Divine Comedy* to match it, the words of Beatrice to Dante in the Earthly Paradise: 'Knewest thou not that here man is happy?'   Nausicaa says to Odysseus, her last words,

Farewell, stranger guest.   That even in your own land you may remember me!   For thou owest the price of thy life to me, the first.

That is all she says.   It is so wonderful in its delicacy, that the answer of Odysseus, though a masterpiece of tact, jars a little, as it could not but jar, no answer being really possible.   Only the very greatest poets can do this kind of thing.   Ophelia's 'No more but so?' may be set beside Nausicaa's farewell.   The critic is afraid to touch words like these, they are so alive and sensitive.   They are as full of mysterious meaning as life itself.   Shakespeare is a great master in this kind of simplicity.   But the Greeks are nearly all masters in it.   It is only achieved by a perfect skill in the use of language; and it is really rather childish to think of the Greeks as lighting on these effects by a series of happy accidents or 'a perfect instinct for the right word', as I have seen it expressed.   The instinct will not give you the word; it will only tell you the word is right when you have found it.   No doubt there is something in the genius of the Greek tongue, which is at once precise and plastic, that helps its writers in their constant aim at a pregnant simplicity. But the genius of a language is the genius of the people as expressed in their language. And so the question, as it affects the Greeks, remains to be answered.

Suppose we take

I loved you, Atthis, once. . .

from Sappho ; the mere

Thus ended the Sicilian Affair

with which Thucydides closes his harrowing account of the Athenian disasters in the West ; the at first sight almost infantile saying of Plato :

The bad things are more than the good;

the remark which Herodotus makes about King Candaules :

He happened to be in love with his own wife—

these phrases are all alike in being perfectly simple, but in each case the effect is quite different. One has to say that Sappho is tender, and Thucydides grimly reticent, and Plato profound, and Herodotus witty ; and that, apparently, to capture Greek simplicity we shall have to cast our net pretty wide. A study like the present does not permit of that. But, without attempting a definition, one may set down certain elements of the problem. I am moved to take Herodotus for a text, because he is never anything but simple, and because he more than any other Greek writer has a reputation for *naiveté*. It is worth enquiring how far the reputation is justified.

It is rapidly disappearing, and may now perhaps be regarded as a survival from a time which read the classics incuriously. The impression that Herodotus is a simple, garrulous fellow (rather of the Izaak Walton type, or even like Sir John Mandeville) is all wrong. Some modern critics are on the verge of calling him Voltairean. The innocent-looking, childlike simplicity of his style is only part of his method of a great artist. The mind it expresses is perhaps not a very profound one; but it is certainly neither timid nor slow. It is on the contrary extraordinarily alert and searching. Herodotus is indeed an extremely emancipated person. Although he was not an Ionian, and although he disparages the Ionians, he has crystallized the sceptical, *insouciant* Ionian spirit better than any other writer we know.

Listen to him upon Helen, about whom the Attic writers always speak with a certain awe.

'In the next generation (the Persians say) Alexander the son of Priam, having come to hear of these matters, was willing that he should get a wife out of Greece by carrying her off, being well assured in his own mind that there would be no requital to be made; for the Greeks made none either. So he carried off Helen. Then the Greeks determined first of all to send messengers to demand Helen back, and to ask satisfaction for the rape. But when they brought forward these claims the Persians on their part brought forward the rape of Medea, saying that the Greeks had neither given compensation nor given her up when they were asked, and yet looked for compensation now from them!   Up to this time, then, (they say) nothing more had happened than carryings off of women on both sides ; but hereafter the Greeks were gravely to blame. For their expedition into Asia was made before the Persian invasion of Greece.   As for the carrying off of women, they are of opinion that it is wrong ; but *after* they are carried away, to insist upon vengeance is silly—a sensible man will pay no attention to them. Obviously, if they had not wanted to be abducted, they would not have been.   When the women were being captured from Asia the Persians disregarded the matter.   But the Greeks gathered together a mighty host and afterwards came to Asia and put down the glory of Priam ; for the sake of a Lacedaemonian woman.'

If the reader objects that this is what the Persians say, he may listen to Herodotus himself.   Helen, the Egyptian priests maintained, had never been to Troy, but was in Egypt all the time; it was only her wraith that went to Troy.   Herodotus says :

'I am inclined to believe them, for these reasons :— If Helen had been in Troy, she would have been given back to the Greeks, whether Alexander liked it or not. For Priam and his relations were not quite so moon-struck as to be prepared to risk their lives and the lives of their children, in order that Alexander might go on living with Helen.   Suppose at first they did agree to this, yet after not only many of the other Trojans fell in battle with the Greeks, but also—if we follow the account of the epic poets—two or three or more of Priam's own sons always got killed—when things like this began to happen I suspect that Priam would have given Helen back to the Achaeans, even if he had been living with her himself. . . .'

This is not the tone of the Romantic poets:

There! they were wrong, as wrong as men could be;
For, as I think, they found it such delight
To see fair Helen going through their town:
Yea, any little common thing she did
(As stooping to pick a flower) seem'd so strange,
So new in its great beauty, that they said;
" Here we will keep her living in this town,
Till all burns up together".

Compared with that, and with the words of the Trojan Elders in the *Iliad*, the language of Herodotus appears almost cynical. It is not really so. But there are two temptations he cannot resist: the temptation of the critic (specially attractive for the slightly mischievous Ionian spirit) to prick romantic bubbles; and the temptation which besets nearly every master of style to show what he could do, if he cared to be provocative and controversial.

Thus :—

'If then I am right about that, the Ionians are wrong in their ideas about Egypt. If on the other hand it is they who are right . . . then I undertake to show that neither they nor the Hellenes know how to count.'

How unfair that is, but how effective! Herodotus of course did not know how to reason according to the rules of Formal Logic, and therefore did not realize how scandalously he was breaking them. But he knows how to deal with an opponent.

'When Hecataeus the historian retailed his genealogy in Thebes and linked his descent to a god in the twelfth generation, the priests of Zeus did to him exactly what they did to me, although I did not retail my genealogy.'

The neatness of that little thrust at the end is delightful.   Chaucer, who, although he writes in so different a medium, is not unlike Herodotus in many things, has the same talent for a demure, innocence-pretending satire.   Here is another example of it :—

'It was not at all the custom of the Persians before his time to consort with their sisters. Cambyses however fell in love with one of his and wished to marry her. But conceiving that this would be an unusual thing to do, he summoned the King's Judges and asked them whether there was any law which allowed any one who liked to marry his sister. The King's Judges are Selected Men among the Persians, and hold their office till death, or till they are found out doing something wrong. These Judges administer the law, and interpret the traditional code for the Persians, and everything is referred to them. Well, when Cambyses put his question, they returned an answer which was at once constitutional and safe. They said that they could not discover a law which permitted a man to marry his sister, but that they *had* discovered one which enacted that the King of the Persians may do anything he likes.'

Another anecdote of the same sardonic quality relates to the Aeacidae, who were the patron-heroes or local Saints of Aegina. The Thebans asked the Aeginetans to help them in a war they were having with the Athenians.

'The Aeginetans said that they would send them the Aeacidae to be their helpers. The Thebans, trusting that the Aeacidae would fight for them, renewed the war, and were roughly handled by the Athenians. So they sent once more to the Aeginetans, and gave them back the Aeacidae, and asked for some men instead.'

Reading passages like these, one begins to feel that the simplicity of Herodotus implicates a number of things. But it may be said (and often is said in equivalent words) "Look at his philosophy; look at his criticism of life. Could anything be more childish?" I suppose that Herodotus' philosophy and religion and criticism of life (so far as he possesses such things at all) would be difficult of defence or even of statement in set, academic terms. But I have to confess that I get exactly the same impression from the moralizing passages as I do from those I have quoted, the impression that he is not so simple as he looks. There is, for instance, the famous lament of Xerxes. Xerxes gloried when he saw at a glance the multitude of his armies and his ships; but after a little, he wept. Artabanus questioned him, and he replied:

'"As I made reckoning, it came over me with a sudden pang how short is human life, seeing that of all this folk not one will be living a hundred years hence."

'The other said "There are sadder things in life than that. In our little lives there is no man so happy, here or anywhere, who will not often have the thought that he would rather be dead than alive. For misfortunes fall, and diseases confound us, and make life that is short seem long. Therefore is death the dearest refuge for man from the malady of living, and the Wrath of God is manifest in this, that he has let us taste the sweetness of life."'

It is open to us to call this an inadequate view of life, not forgetting that we have still to invent an adequate one. But to call it superficial is a cheap and modern impertinence. It is not of the surface, but is distilled from the roots of human experience. One would like to know what Mr. Hardy thinks of it. We know (Mr. Hardy reminding us) what Gloucester thinks in *King Lear*:

As flies to wanton boys are we to the gods;
They kill us for their sport.

True, Herodotus has no pretensions to be a philosopher. He is a 'Maker of Logoi', a professional Teller of Tales, an artist in the spoken word. He is much more than that, of course; but he is that. He is a popularizer, in the noble ancient way. He is content to express popular morality, the hard experience of the long generations, in language which the simple man will understand. Not an easy thing to do, certainly ; but a thing which, when it is done as well as Herodotus does it, rings in the mind for ever.

Herodotus at least understood the artistic uses of simplicity. This invites to the larger question, whether the Greek love of simple style is a mere artistic fashion or preference. I do not know why we should be offended if it were so. But in fact it is a great deal more than that. It follows the natural bias of the Greek mind, and goes directly with the Greek attitude to life. Regarding this attitude people say all kinds of things, but all agree that it differs from the general modern attitude in a certain directness or immediacy of approach. The Greek temper deals with life in a singularly free and unembarrassed way, earnest to see things just as they are, and not afraid of the truth when it does appear. It is eminently a positive and reasonable spirit—not coldly reasonable, however. Out of it springs a striving to reduce the statement of every problem and situation to its simplest terms. There burns everywhere in Greek literature a hatred of illusion, of pretence, of affectation, of rhetoric and sentimentality, of prejudice and onesidedness. The Greek mind was filled with a passion for reality seizing not only the understanding but the imagination as well. See how this emotion invades the subtlest speculations of Greek philosophy. The search is for the Thing Itself, for Something more real and permanent than the changeful, crumbling things of sense; the hope is to create, and *work*, a Perfect State, that will outlast all existing constitutions. And the Greek was most plainly an artist in this, that he thought Beauty the most real thing in the world; also the wisest, the most sane and healing. The Beautiful is the True and the Good. What a thing to believe, I mean to believe effectively! But if it is believed, observe that the distinction between realism and idealism in art becomes practically unmeaning. For beauty being the most real thing in the world, the search for beauty, which is the ideal, is at the same time the search for reality. The Greek criticism of Zola (or any one like him) would be that he was a bad artist; not because he was working in the wrong spirit—for he sought the truth— but because he had found the truth ugly. That is in effect what Aristophanes says about Euripides.

The desire of simplicity being so rooted in the Greek temperament, we want to know how it operated. When we come to consider this, we are at once in the midst of difficulties. For Greek art is not always simple. It is often complex and elaborate to a degree of which modern art is not patient nor very often competent.

The structure of a Greek choric ode, for example, is a technical miracle. And the language is answerably ornate, involved, and allusive—extremely difficult. Think of the first chorus of the *Agamemnon*; it is as hard as Meredith. What then are we to say about this? Is it simply that, while the majority of Greek writers aim at simplicity, there are many who have a predilection for an involved and enigmatic style? That looks an acceptable answer, till one discovers a singular thing. In Greek literature it is not so much authors who are simple or the reverse as styles. So that, if you were an epic poet you wrote simply; whereas if you made choral lyrics you must write in ornate, allusive diction and elaborate metre. That is to say, there was a traditional epic style, which was simple—the Homeric style; and a traditional style for the choric ode—the style elaborated by Pindar and Aeschylus.

We moderns hardly understand what a traditional style is. The nearest thing to it we have in English is no doubt the Ballad style. One can see Coleridge and Rossetti following a very definite convention in *The Rime of the Ancient Mariner* and *The King's Tragedy*. But if anyone were to tell a short story in any diction and any metre he pleased and call it a Ballad, no one would raise any objection at all. You may write epic in the manner of Milton, or of *Sigurd the Volsung*, or of Mr. Doughty, or in some private manner of your own; and still it is an epic if you choose to call it so. The Greeks of the Great Age would not have understood this. They deemed of Art as one, a common labour. They thought of poetry as a great cathedral building through the ages, or an endless tapestry which could be worked upon indefinitely. If you did not follow the design of your predecessor, but introduced some eccentricity of your own, you were spoiling everything. As if, Plato says, a man were to paint the eyes of a statue purple, merely because he regarded purple as the prettiest colour. We do not think of all the poets labouring at a common inherited task ; the poets themselves do not think so now. They refuse to be bound by any convention in subject or style. They are indeed especially eager to escape the appearance of conventionality ; and everyone is as aggressively original as he can be.

Ruskin, here, is on the Greek side :—

' In all base schools of art ',—I should be content to say, in other schools—' the craftsman is dependent for his bread on originality ; that is to say, on finding in himself some fragment of isolated faculty, by which his work may be recognized as distinct from that of other men. We are ready enough to take delight in our little doings, without any such stimulus ; what must be the effect of the popular applause which continually suggests that the little thing we can separately do is as excellent as it is singular ! . . . In all great schools of art these conditions are exactly reversed. An artist is praised in these, not for what is different in him from others ; . . . but only for doing most strongly what all are endeavouring ; and for contributing . . . to some great achievement, to be completed by the unity of multitudes, and the sequence of ages.'

This doctrine the Greeks applied to poetry as well as to the other arts which are principally in Ruskin's mind. They said : If you choose a certain kind of subject, you ought to treat it in a certain way, discovered by the experience of ages to be the best.   If you try a manner of your own, you will do it at your peril.   For there is a harmony of matter and manner not to be discovered in a day.   Instead of labouring to perfect that, you are experimenting with a new combination.   We believe this to be a mistake, and a kind of impiety as well.

The impiety was not simply to the great poets dead ; it was also in a way an impiety towards the gods themselves.   For poetry in Greece, and all Greek art, was in its origin a vital part of religion, from which it was never able wholly to sever itself.   If it had, we may believe it would have died.   At least it would have been something so different that we cannot even imagine it.   What would the Attic Drama or the odes of Pindar, what even would the epic have been like, torn from their religious setting ?   Greek poetry is not unique in having a religious origin ; what is unique in it is the completeness and the consecutiveness of the tradition which takes us back to its beginnings.   The earliest poetry is, by all the evidence, a form of charm or spell.   This *carmen* is the accompaniment of a magical dance.   It is a kind of interpretation or description of the dance, which has always a mimetic or semi-dramatic character.   It comes to the same thing if we say the dance is a kind of enactment or dramatization of the chant.   The dance is performed by the entire community or 'tribe' of able and qualified dancers.   Hence poetry is in its beginnings choral ; a very important conclusion.   The poet is at first the leader or precentor of the chorus.   In time he becomes, as it were, professional, and steps out of the chorus, to sing to them now instead of with them.   And so by degrees we come to the poet living in his 'ivory tower' and

> *Singing hymns unbidden,*
> *Till the world is wrought*
> *To sympathy with hopes and fears it heeded not.*

It has been largely disputed whether religion was evolved out of magic, or magic is a depravation of religion. The very question suggests their connexion. In primitive communities the association seems inextricable. So whether we say that the dance-song (which is the protoplasm of poetry) has a religious, or whether we say it has a magical character, we cannot be far out. Some call it 'magico-religious' and feel safe. It is communal or 'tribal', thus possessing an inclusiveness in one direction and an exclusiveness in the other quite foreign to our notions of poetry. It is inclusive in this, that it demands (with certain obvious exceptions) all the members of the community for its performance. It is exclusive in so far as it is restricted to the community. The restriction is very jealous. The dance is a secret, and on the preservation of the secret knowledge depends the safety, and even the existence, of the 'tribe'. For the dance is a kind of spell to bind the unseen powers in the service of the dancers; and if others learn the manner of it, how shall they be prevented from drawing the gods to their side? Naturally the tendency is to make the dance complicated and, as it were, esoteric; while of course the words accompanying and interpreting the dance will follow a parallel development. Ancient religion is full of 'mysteries', which are ceremonies intelligible only to the initiated. The core of such a 'mystery' is almost invariably found to be a sacred dance with accompaniment of a ritual chant or Hymn. So long as it is genuinely a part of the ceremony, the Hymn will tend to be cryptic and baffling to the profane. It will not be published at all, until it has lost its power as a spell ; and then it will be made simple for all the world.

The choral song, then, is the oldest form of poetry. In Greece it remained undivorced from the ritual dance, and was never, so far as we know, chanted except on some occasion of a religious colour. Its subject remained the myth or 'sacred story', which was but the spoken part of the ritual. Every *pagus* and little state of ancient Hellas had its special, guarded cere-monial, in which the central part was played by a dancing and singing company who celebrated the local 'sacred story'. We hear constantly of these choruses. A religious chorus in the service of Dionysus forms the heart of Attic Drama. The *Frogs* of Aristophanes has a chorus of *Mystae*, initiates of Iacchus, who came to be identified with Dionysus. They sing like this :—

> *Spirit, Spirit, lift the shaken*
> *Splendour of thy tossing torches !*
> *All the meadow flashes, scorches :*
> *Up, Iacchus, and awaken !*
> *Come, thou star that bringest light*
> *To the darkness of our rite,*
> *Till thine old men leap as young men, leap with every*
> *thought forsaken*
> *Of the dulness and the fear*
> *Left by many a circling year :*
> *Let thy red light guide the dances*
> *Where thy banded youth advances*
> *To be joyous by the blossoms of the mere !*

The solemn hieratic note is unmistakable. This is

truly the language of initiates, who are people possessed of and by a secret, wonderful knowledge. The note recurs in the choric odes of Euripides' *Bacchanals*, a play which dramatizes with much fidelity and 'realism' the very ritual from which the Tragic Drama sprang. It is the Wisdom of the god's chosen ones that is praised, for instance here:—

> *Knowledge, we are not foes!*
>   *I seek thee diligently;*
> *But the world with a great wind blows,*
>   *Shining, and not from thee;*
> *Blowing to beautiful things,*
>   *On, amid dark and light,*
> *Till life through the trammellings*
>   *Of Laws that are not the Right,*
> *Breaks, clean and pure, and sings*
>   *Glorying to God in the height!*

From the old guarded Mysteries of Eleusis, which it was death to reveal, are wafted echoes of strange import:

> *Lift up your hearts, ye Initiate!   The God is saved,*

and

> *We have found, we rejoice together,*

and

> *I have escaped an ill thing, I have found a better.*

The literature of Pythagoreanism and Orphism is full of such mysterious sentences. They help us to realize the kind of atmosphere in which the choral lyric grew up. We shall not overstate anything in calling it a ritualistic atmosphere; and perhaps I shall be understood if I call the traditional style of the choral ode a ritualistic style.

One has only to look at Pindar and the Dramatists to perceive this. No poet ever felt the dignity of his calling more than Pindar ; not Ronsard nor Milton nor Victor Hugo. But Pindar was not wholly unjustified in regarding himself as a kind of god ; for he *was* one, and his fellow countrymen so regarded him. Tracked far enough back, the poet merges with the prophet, the priest, the king, the god, to form that strange, indistinct figure, the magician who rules the primitive community. Something of this halo of a former divinity still lingered in Pindar's time about the brows of the poet, or at least of a poet derived as lineally as he from the old Leader of the Dance. Every one of his Odes breathes a deep sense of the solemnity of its occasion, even when (as some critic remarks) the occasion is somebody's victory in a mule-race. Pindar, one of the most conservative of men or at least of poets, and certainly one of the greatest of artists, in a wonderful way crystallizes this religious atmosphere. Read one of the Odes, and you must acknowledge that that high, cryptic style is made for the celebration of some gorgeous ritual. What Pindar himself says is this : *In a quiver under my arm are many swift arrows that speak to those who have the Knowledge, but need interpretation to the multitude.* That is exactly the attitude of the hierophant : *odi profanum uolgus et arceo.*

The choric odes in the Tragedies are also composed in the ritualistic style. Who has not felt, especially in Aeschylus, but not rarely in Sophocles and Euripides as well, something mysterious and pontifical in the language of the choruses? The Tragic Chorus is itself indeed a company of sacrosanct beings, partakers in a solemn service, initiate persons. They are so in virtue

of their function as Sacred Dancers about the altar of
the god.   Hence their words, as Mr. F. M. Cornford has
observed, often seem to come from another world than
this of ours, remoter and happier, out of space and time
—the world which is felt as real by those who share in
the ecstasy of some divine revelation.   Their singing
is all of divine persons, gods and godlike kings and
queens of old days, and in a kind of veiled, oracular
speech.   This is an instance of it, taken from the
Agamemnon of Aeschylus :

μίμνει γὰρ φοβερὰ παλίνορτος
οἰκονόμος δολία μνάμων, μῆνις τεκνόποινος.

' For there abideth a fearful, back-springing, home-
keeping, crafty, unforgetting, Wrath child-avenging.'
What does it mean ?   Well, it gradually becomes clear
in the course of the play.   But assuredly language like
this requires ' interpretation to the vulgar '.   The choric
odes of Aeschylus are admittedly more obscure—the
word is properly used in this sense—than those of
Sophocles, and the odes of Sophocles again than those
of Euripides.   That is what we should expect.   The
evolution was from a ritualistic to an ever plainer and
more popular style.

   But—' Homer is simple, and the Homeric Poems stand
at the beginning of Greek literature.'   What does this
prove, however ?   Not that the epos is older in *kind*
than the choral song.   On the contrary Homer, who
often refers to some dancing and singing chorus, clearly
regards his own art as something very much more
recent and developed ; he says that men praise the
song that rings newest in their ears.   Besides, it is
evident that a bard of the Homeric sort is not in the

very least a primitive person. He is really more of a professional than any modern poet would like to think himself. Yet the manner of his evolution is fairly clear; he too is the descendant of the *choragos* or chorus-leader. A chorus must in the nature of things get itself a leader, some one to strike up the tune and lead off the dance. As the ritual becomes more elaborate and perhaps (as in Greece at least it became) more definitely beautiful, it takes more and more skill and special knowledge to lead it—takes a professional in fact. This is not simple conjecture. Demodocus in the *Odyssey* sings the Loves of Ares and Aphrodite, the lay being danced by a choir of young Phaeaecians, while he harps in their midst and acts as their *choragos*. The lay itself is epic and in hexameter. The epos is here seen at a middle point in its development from the choric song. When the bard has entirely severed his connexion with the choir, he will become the epic poet, chanting his verses to an audience which has now nothing to do but listen.

The epos then was formed by the severance of the hymn from its ritual. That was a process of secularization; and in general we may say that the history of Greek poetry is the history of its progressive secularization. It is what we should expect of the Greeks. They were not an irreligious race, but the contrary. They could never be contented, however, with a religion of mere emotion or unreasoned conviction, nor feed their spirit on mere passionate assertion. They must frame some kind of theory about the gods (not dogma), which was capable of an argued defence. The appeal to reason created philosophy, which set itself early to criticize the assumptions of popular theology. Although there was, according to Plato, an ancient quarrel between Philosophy and Poetry (for the poets clung to the dear exploded legends), yet the speculations of the early thinkers did gradually influence the minds of all men. But far more important for poetry was a force which is bound up with its very existence. Poetry, like every other art, can only develop by asserting the law of its own being, which is not the law that governs the existence of religion. Though art may work in the service of religion, the service must be voluntary. The moment that the chain is felt, inspiration dies. It was a great thing for Greece and for the world that poetry so early asserted its independence. It is completely asserted in Homer, and of course in other later poets. In spirit it is asserted even in the choral lyric, although there something of the old subordination remains: the association with a ritual dance, the elevated and enigmatic language.

The appeal from the closed circle of the religious society to the 'profane' or general public requires a change to the use of the common idiom to make it effective or even intelligible. So poetry moved in the direction of plainness and simplicity to the extent in which it moved away from religion. Thus Homer is perfectly simple. The same may be said of Sappho and Alcaeus. The difficulty of translating them (which is great) does not arise from any involution or obscurity of style, but from other causes, one of them being the dialect. They are simple because, although their metres were probably choral dance-measures to begin with, they have separated themselves from the choir and sing alone their personal joys and sorrows. Again, elegiac poetry is not choral, and has vindicated for itself the freedom and directness of Homer. Iambic poetry holds a peculiar position. The metre was originally the measure of one of those obscene ritual dances which come so frequently, and to our minds so incongruously, in ancient religion. The earliest iambic poetry (of which only fragments remain) is violently abusive and satirical; and this trait is derived from the ritual, where the dance was combined with much indecent jesting and abuse of persons. We clearly have to rank the iambics of Archilochus and Hippônax with the simple forms of Greek poetry, for their *style* is quite simple. Their language is hard, being a kind of special vocabulary, full of comic, abusive words.

The iambic parts of Attic Drama need a word to themselves. A distinction must first be drawn between the manner of Tragedy and that of Comedy. The Comic trimeter is free and conversational; the Tragic written in a special diction widely removed from ordinary speech. This diction moves in the direction of simplicity from Aeschylus through Sophocles to Euripides. At least this is broadly true, though the statement requires a little guarding. Aeschylus can be simple enough in syntax, while the language is stiff with gorgeous elaboration; as in *Prometheus Bound*. Sophocles is very subtle in his management of syntax, but incredibly sparing of ornament, and constantly seeking effects which triumphantly escape, but just escape, the prosaic. The diction of Euripides is in some ways the most conventional of the three; but he is less preoccupied with style probably than Aeschylus, certainly than Sophocles, and is more readily understood than either. But the important thing is that the Tragic Style is traditional; as much part of the Tragic convention as the Chorus or the use of masks.   Perhaps it was the most vital part of all, for it was the discovery and perfecting of it which made Tragedy as a literary form possible.   Mr. F. M. Cornford in his book on the Origin of Attic Comedy has made it seem probable that Greek Tragedy and Comedy had a common source in a mummery of the type still performed in outlying parts of Europe and notably in Northern Greece.   It is a kind of tragi-comedy in which the hero is 'killed', restored to life, and united or reunited to his bride. It was the pathetic element in this performance, the slaying of the hero and the lamentation for his untimely end, which developed into Tragedy.   The Aristophanic Comedy retains and enlarges the joyous ending of it all.   But both Tragedy and Comedy were evolved in the service and atmosphere of religion, and may be regarded as elaborated rituals; more accurately, as elaborated versions or parts of one old ritual.   The least knowledge of ancient religion, and particularly of the Dionysiac religion with its dual character, will keep us from wondering why one version is solemn, and the other obscene and grotesque.   It is Comedy which best preserves the 'satyric' tone of the original mummery or folk-play; Aristotle himself implies this. Tragedy, in winning its way to its 'excellent serious-ness', had to purge the traditional style of the elements which made against seriousness, while keeping (like all Greek art) what it could—the sense and pressure of a religious occasion.   So we may say that the iambic portions of Tragedy are written, like choric odes, in the ritualistic style.   The language is grave, lofty, serious; often enigmatic and 'ironical'.   Has the reader noticed how often the speakers in Greek

Tragedy accuse one another of talking in riddles? No doubt this has a dramatic value. But it is really a convention turned, in the Greek way, to an artistic use; a convention of the ritualistic style.

As to Greek prose, although it became an artistic medium much later than poetry, and did not have its roots entangled in ritual, it did on the whole work steadily in the direction of clearness and that pellucid 'Attic' quality which has become proverbial. It is rare to find an involved or difficult style in classical prose. (I am not in this essay considering post-classical literature at all.) Heraclitus writes in an oracular manner which represents the esoteric style of the Wise Man which he purposely makes unintelligible to everybody except himself and his disciples. Again, the speeches in Thucydides are hard. This is because they are written in a style, modified from Gorgias, which was strongly influenced by study of the poets. If we regard the *History* as constructed on the lines of a Tragedy—a view for which there is much to be said—the speeches may be taken as corresponding to the choric odes. But such exceptions as Heraclitus and Thucydides yield do not affect the general current of Greek prose in the direction of clearness and simplicity—*studied* simplicity. Aristotle says that clearness is the chief virtue of style; and that is the Greek view.

In the light of this enquiry into origins, Greek simplicity assumes the aspect of a victory over tradition. Yet in another sense the tradition was victorious in defeat. For it inspires the new style with—what shall I say?—the suggestion of great hidden meanings, of some divine and wonderful secret, such as the ritualistic style was designed to convey. How often in reading Greek poetry are we brought up by a line of perfect simplicity which moves us in a way we cannot measure or explain!   These lines are most frequent, I think, in Attic Tragedy, whose style I have called ritualistic, but might just as well have called simple, so hard is it to mark the boundary. What is the exact value for the imagination of this line in the *Agamemnon* :

> ἔστιν θάλασσα· τίς δέ νιν κατασβέσει ;
> *'There is the sea, and who shall dry it up?'*

or of this in the *Prometheus* :

> HERMES. *'Success would make thee intolerable.*
> PROMETHEUS, *'Ah me . . .'?*

It is Aeschylus again who says

> *'Alone of the gods Death craveth no gift'.*

The blind Oedipus in Sophocles says

> *'O light that is as darkness, once, surely, thou wert mine'.*
> ὦ φῶς ἀφεγγὲς, πρόσθε πού ποτ' ἦσθ' ἐμόν.

This also is from Sophocles :

> *'None is so much in love with life as the old man'.*

Electra in Euripides says over the murdered Aegisthus whom she desires to curse :

> *'I am ashamed, but I wish to speak too'.*
> αἰσχύνομαι μὲν, βούλομαι δ'εἰπεῖν ὅμως.

An old man in Euripides complains:

> '*An old man is but a shadow and a noise of words*'.
> φωνὴ καὶ σκιὰ γέρων ἀνήρ.

Praxithea in the lost *Erechtheus*, in yielding her child to be sacrificed for the saving of Athens, utters a cry which I will not even attempt to translate:

> χρῆσθ', ὦ πολῖται, τοῖς ἐμοῖς λοχεύμασιν,
> σώζεσθε, νικᾶτ·'

One could go on for long quoting lines like that. They are like pools of clear water reflecting the mystery and infinite depths of starry skies.

Note

The metrical translations of Euripides are Gilbert Murray's.

LUCRETIUS

I HAVE been reading Baudelaire, and I think I now understand why Lucretius seems to us different from every other poet of antiquity. He has the malady which finds its most conscious expression in the *Fleurs du Mal*. This malady I do not think is well described by *ennui*; the ancients were familiar enough with that; what is called the Silver Age of Latin literature is heavy with ennui. A more subtle and poignant irritation of the spirit plagues these two poets. Its true nature is perhaps already plain to the reader, or should partially transpire in discussion. But it would be very hard to define; at least I have never seen a very satisfactory definition of it. So I content myself with some indications positive enough to justify the parallel, which at first has an appearance of being grotesque or forced. No doubt the spiritual history of Lucretius was widely different from that of Baudelaire, and their interests were different. But in the end—and this is the sole point I would make— they were unhappy with the same kind of un- happiness.

One likes to think of Lucretius, as little urban in his sympathies as Wordsworth himself, spending his childhood in the fields rather than the town. We may imagine him staying at some country mansion

(mansion or farmhouse) in a cleft of the Apennines overlooking the Campagna, habitable then with vine and olive. Here he had come when Rome became unbearable in autumn ; and here the child wandering among the embrowned hill-pastures, the dry boulder-strewn water-courses, and the scarlet-oaks would hear and see many unforgettable things. Unforgotten at least by him. Are there anywhere, or anywhere out of Homer, such descriptions as his ? They have the miraculous quality—the Homeric quality—of making us see everything as if for the first time and in the morning of creation. Add to this, that they have the conscientious exactness of Wordsworth. So we see the cast skin of the adder aflutter upon the bramble thorn ; the great flock of sheep feeding on the hill and moving so gradually as to look from the valley motionless as a patch of snow ; the coloured shells left by the retreating tide in a thin wavy line for miles along the sand ; the tempest in the mountain forest when the boughs gride together until at last the flame blossoms forth a sudden flower upon the branch. The memory of these things stayed. They remained with him through that obscure fever of the spirit or the nerves which beset him when he wrote his poem. The descriptive passages in it could not have been written except out of the love, the observation and the memories of a lifetime. It is perhaps an added proof of this that one may trace— or is it only a fancy ?—the workings of the fever, a certain wistfulness or nostalgia in these parts. Even in the wonderful fifth book, so redolent of the open air, I seem to find a touch of the convalescent's eagerness for freedom and freshness.

Oh, feet of a fawn to the greenwood fled,
  Alone in the grass and the loveliness,
Leap of the Hunted, no more in dread. . . .

But this note would be absent at first.

Not only was it things seen that impressed his childhood, but also things more than natural. Here, away from the markets and streets, the simple and affecting old Italian religion could still convince. Who was that piping so far up the gorge? Faunus or a shepherd? He knew that supernatural powers had been busy about his own life as far back as he could remember. There were the Powers who taught him to eat and drink; those who gave him bodily strength; *Levana*, who helped him to rise from the ground. By the central hearth stood the little images of the household gods, to which the elder members of the family were so greatly attached. Then there were the 'greater' gods, in whose hands lay the final administration of the universe; who were duly worshipped indeed, but with a less intimate sense of nearness to the worshipper. And Silvans and Fauns, startling with sudden outcries the stillness of lonely pastoral places; fair-haired Pomona in the orchard, Ceres in the corn; a rustic Saturn and Mars; Vertumnus and Anna Perenna of the Turning Year. Finally there was that mysterious other self, the *genius*, with whose existence his own was in some unexplained way bound up. With such an upbringing an imaginative child would thrill to every intimation of the divine. It touched him at so many points of his being, this presence behind the veil of the visible and audible. I think Lucretius, although he ceased to believe in 'religion' as such, never quite lost this instinctive feeling of a significance in things not apparent on their surface. Was not the world continually moving to new, unguessed combinations of atoms? In the depths of a great wood the silence would sometimes invade his heart with a thrill of unreasonable Panic terror. It was indeed just this imaginative nearness to nature which enabled him to paint the conditions of primitive man with such arresting realism.

'Natural piety' then Lucretius possessed, and as abundantly as any poet has possessed it. It must at first have recommended to him that widely different thing from which a boy could not clearly distinguish it —the piety of the average rustic. But paganism, the religion of the *pagus*, whatever a certain kind of idealism may conjecture, was not then any more than now on the whole a blithe or attractive sentiment. There were too many *laruae* and *lemures*, malicious ghosts to frighten a child. The peasant women could tell him such stories of haunted chambers and murdered travellers! Stories also of the world after death, the dismal realm of Orcus. All manner of wretched fancies and beliefs marred the joy of existence in the remoter valleys; every now and then the inhabitants ran to perform rites, better left undescribed, of the kind that will often survive so long in places where the current of life has flowed in the same channel for many generations. It may be that Lucretius was a little touched besides by that habitual pessimism of the husbandman to which at the end of the second book he has given sombre and resonant expression. At any rate the gloomy and terrifying character of the thing men called their religion must have awakened early his vivid

human sympathies. Rome was worst of all. There
an unimaginative rationalism, the fruit of a half-
assimilated culture, had merely destroyed most of
what was touching and amiable in the ancient national
religion without substituting anything except some
Oriental superstitions chiefly compounded of dirt,
delirium, and exciting promises, and a half-hearted
belief in Chance. Lucretius, who has a sincerity that
almost frightens one, could never be content with this.
Every reader has felt the peculiar thrill of the famous
passage in which the poet cries out against religion as
the grand enemy of the truth, and of human happiness
which depends upon realization of the truth. Yet
Lucretius is not irreligious, while to call him atheistic
is to misapprehend his system, which admitted the
existence of a divine principle and only denied its
active interest in human affairs. Though he has dis-
pensed with the gods of popular belief, he has not rid
himself of the emotions which for most people make
some form of religion indispensable. He is like Plato
in the way he feels the fascination and (to their minds)
sometimes sinister beauty of that mythology which is
the immortal part of the old-world beliefs. It was in
fact the very intensity of the religious sentiment in
Lucretius which lent such vehemence to his protest
against the current religion. The thing is a preoccupation to him. In spite of his perpetual appeal
to reason he has the instinctive preference of the artist
—and the religious—for moods rather than ideas. ' He
was a true poet, and of the devil's party without
knowing it.'

The consolation of religion thus set aside, what other
was left to him? Philosophy? No doubt in time his

philosophy came to be everything to Lucretius. But that was only after it had become a second nature to him ; at first it was, to him as to any other young man, chiefly an intellectual pastime. As to his choice between systems, it was practically limited to the two contending schools of thought which had come into special prominence since Alexander's death—the Stoic and the Epicurean. That he embraced the philosophy of Epicurus with such fervour of conviction will seem intelligible enough to anyone who admits that we choose a creed by instinct and defend it afterwards on principle. Stoicism is a very noble creed. It has even a heroic quality, which, in a character like Marcus, makes our standards seem a little self-indulgent by contrast. But it does contain something antipathetic to the poetical temperament. (There is indeed Lucan, master at least of a fine poetical rhetoric). The reason is that Stoicism appeals so little to the sensuous imagination. In this (as in some other respects) it resembles the philosophy of Kant. If you can imagine the *Critique of Pure Reason* in poetry . . . but the thing is plainly impossible. So it is with Stoicism. It has the bare sublimity of a great sea-cliff, impressive but a little oppressive as well. Lucretius, with the temperament of the poet rather than the philosopher, would naturally be drawn to a system which made much of the mere pleasantness of living ; and this Epicureanism did. Valuing sensations for their own sake, particularly in their more delicate forms and *nuances* ; and then, on the other hand, so trenchantly clear and uncompromising merely as a speculation, it would seem to reconcile two occasionally quarrelsome tendencies in himself: and this, without the sort of conviction which only comes with the ripening of experience, is sufficient to account for the choice of a dogma at an age when opinions are lightly adopted and not too consistently maintained.

For this reason I think that those who begin their study of Lucretius with his philosophical opinions will never understand how he came to hold them at all. For this philosopher happening to be a poet, in the natural order of events he was a poet before he became a philosopher. To suppose the contrary is to postulate him a psychological portent. In order then to follow the direction of his development we must set out from the earlier stage, his period of comparatively unreflecting submission to impressions. Indeed it is in general clear that before a man makes the sacrifices that Lucretius made to his ideal of intellectual honesty he will try a good many things. For Lucretius made sacrifice of his heart. His philosophical opinions!— why, he acquired them as certain sensitive creatures are said to grow a protective shell.

We have seen that he could get no satisfaction in religion. He did get some from the vast and moving spectacle of human progress in the arts of life. He often thought with eager admiration and gratitude of the great benefactors of humanity: Empedocles, Democritus, Epicurus. But after all, what evils this 'progress' had brought in its train! We had spurned the gifts, the 'golden *dicta*', of the wise; and what we had gained in knowledge and in skill we had lost in character. And with it all were we any happier than the savage ancestor routed from his bed of leaves by some chance-roaming brute? It was possible to doubt that.—Well then, the practical life, party politics—he might give himself to that? Alas, he hated politics. And so there appeared to be nothing left but the life of pleasure.

The manner of that life as practised in the last days of the Republic has been described and dwelt upon in many places. By this time had already well begun that Roman luxury which the writers of the Empire have made a monstrous legend. It is no longer possible to accept their account without qualification. On such a subject the great vice of Latin literature—its rhetorical bias—has full play. We have also to take into account that queer disposition of the human soul, especially marked in countries where there is a puritanic tradition and therefore very disconcerting to the moralist, to revel in the details of its own naughtiness. Roman writers are always trying to shock you; and sometimes they positively remind one of an American journalist describing 'society' in New York. We must therefore discount the extent of the evil in the account of Roman writers themselves; its reality we have no right to deny or belittle. The Romans were a people of gross appetites, and their vice was gross and vulgar and ugly. There is really no defensible ground for denying that, and accordingly it must be counted in as part of Lucretius' environment.

Lucretius strikes us as almost excessively sensitive, fastidious; the coarser delights of the average man— *homme sensuel moyen*—seem to affect him with a sick distaste. He is not what anyone would call a full-blooded person. For all that he is profoundly sensuous. He writes on an abstract subject, but his diction is as coloured as Milton's. It was not for nothing that he had these hungry susceptibilities. It would be strange

if they did not at first accept much that he afterwards
rejected with the disgust of a weary experience.   And,
after all, Rome was a great place for a young man to
be in.   He had the feeling of being at the centre of
things.   He met people who were 'in the know' and
'in the swim'.   And certainly in those days life in the
capital was exciting.   The condition of public affairs
having become, as it seemed, quite hopeless, men spent
their lives with the reckless gaiety of gamblers.   Doubtless they argued like the Athenians in Thucydides
when the Plague was upon them: 'it was only natural
that, before it fell, they should have a little pleasure
of their lives'.   Think of Catullus in the heart of this
society, the significance of his experience, the significance of his poetry.   The poetry of the senses, of which
he has given us a typical expression, has always at such
epochs a deep attraction because it is received as a form
of spiritual anodyne.   The *De Rerum Natura* attracted
the most meagre attention on its appearance.   The
reasons for its failure it is unnecessary to discuss here.
Yet there was one thing about it which, other things
being equal, should have made for its success: it was
designed, far more deliberately than anything in Catullus
(who is thinking of his own wound only), to be a
spiritual anodyne.   It is written of purpose to comfort
the sad hearts of men, in particular to rid them of that
fear of the unknown, which he doubtless overestimates
in them—an error natural to one who was not only
imaginative but whose imagination, for a reason, was
somewhat overheated.

Designedly the poem was written for the confirmation
of others; secretly or unconsciously it was written to
console himself.   The least sensitive reader must feel

that Lucretius himself has suffered. We cannot help remembering the story, hinted at rather than told in a single enigmatic sentence of S. Jerome, of a jealous mistress—a love-potion—consequent madness and suicide—the *De Rerum Natura* composed *per interualla insaniae*, in the lucid moments of his malady. All this may be pure legend. But, if it is, it has been moulded like so many other legends by an unerring psychological instinct. Some experience not dissimilar in its essential nature must have happened to Lucretius. I at least cannot get rid of that thought every time I read, for instance, that dreadful conclusion to the fourth book, the cry—is it not?—of one who has been mortally wounded.

'Consider further, that these lovers exhaust their strength and wear themselves quite out, and that their days are passed in the service of another. Meanwhile their substance crumbles away, exchanged for Babylonian tapestries; Duty is neglected, Honour falls sick and lame.—Fair slippers of Sicyon laugh upon *her* feet, yes and great emeralds are set for her with their green light in gold, and the sea-purple vesture is worn threadbare with continual use and drinks the sweat of the amorous body. The heir converts his father's well won thrift into snoods and diadems, sometimes a sweeping pall, or silks of Cos and Alinda—all in vain! since from the bottom of the honeyed spring wells up *some* taste of bitterness to anguish him among the actual flowers— perhaps the remorseful thought that he is passing a life of idle hours and murdering his youth in a shameful passion; or because She has left the shaft of some ambiguous speech that clings to his craving heart like a restless flame; or because the tortured spirit dreams

of meaning glances cast upon another, or traces in
her face the ghost of a traitorous smile. . . .'

Even in Catullus there is nothing more poignant than
this and, despite the veil of the 'third person' in
Lucretius, nothing more personal. And it has something which the poetry of Catullus lacks. Not the
moan of an offended purity, for that is audible enough
in certain passages of Catullus also, and Baudelaire was
quite unfair when he called the lover of Lesbia *poète
brutal et purement épidermique*. But doubtless Catullus
lacks subtlety, as Burns lacks it; and as Sappho and,
in his quite different manner, Lucretius do not. It is
of course not subtlety of art of which I am speaking,
but subtlety of emotion. You may in revenge call
Lucretius morbid; as, for instance, Matthew Arnold did.

It is in this subtlety, and in the peculiar quality of
it, that Lucretius seems to me to approach Baudelaire.
Thus he never speaks of love but with a curious, un-
necessary-seeming violence. It is 'a feeding, flourish-
ing ulcer', 'a vulture tearing at the heart'. This is the
very tone of Baudelaire:

> *J'ai cherché dans l'amour un sommeil oublieux;*
> *Mais l'amour n'est pour moi qu'un matelas d'aiguilles.*

Or read this, put in the mouth of the Poet's mistress:

> *Et, quand je m'ennuîrai de ces farces impies,*
> *Je poserai sur lui ma frêle et forte main;*
> *Et mes ongles, pareils aux ongles des harpies,*
> *Sauront jusqu'à son cœur se frayer un chemin.*
> *Comme un tout jeune oiseau qui tremble et qui palpite,*
> *J'arracherai ce cœur tout rouge de son sein,*
> *Et, pour rassasier ma bête favorite,*
> *Je le lui jetterai par terre avec dédain!*

And here is Lucretius' very metaphor:

—O fureur des cœurs mûrs par l'amour ulcérés!

A passage in the *De Rerum Natura* gives us the pathology of the subject. It is one of the most curious things in ancient literature. The poet seems to begin over and over again in a vain attempt to keep quite calm and objective ; over and over again he seems on the verge of a confession. At brief intervals we hear the recurrent cry, so characteristic of him—*nequiquam*, 'unavailingly!' This passage 'science'? It is not science, it is a human being torturing itself in the name and for the sake of science—a new type of the *Hauton Timorumenos*, sympathetic enough to us, but surely very unexpected in Caesar's Rome.

But consider Lucretius in this light and see how much it explains : for instance, a touch of what in another man would look like cynicism in his attitude to love.

Mon cœur, que tout irrite,
Excepté la candeur de l'antique animal—

He might have put that into echoing hexameters; he did say something very like it. His heart, like Baudelaire's on occasion, yearned back to a simpler, more frankly animal age.

J'aime les souvenirs de ces époques nues,
Dont Phoebus se plaisait à dorer les statues. . . .

He felt 'the call of the wild', if I may use a phrase somewhat vulgarized by repetition. It is even possible perhaps—although he would not have liked to be told so—to detect in him a lurking sympathy with the charming monsters ("Pagan, I regret to say "), Centaurs and Sirens and the like, who *couldn't* have existed because Reason and Epicurus disallow them.—The 'rich prooemion' with which the poem opens—a hymn to that most ancient of goddesses the *Potnia Therôn*, Mother and Queen of the wild creatures—reads almost joyously, like a momentary escape from the habitual tenor of his thoughts and the burden of his mission.

Also it seems less wonderful now that the cry of Lucretius is always for rest, the perfect rest. *Nonne omni somno securius exstat?*—'Is it not more untroubled than any sleep?'

"O man", he makes Nature exclaim, "why dost thou so yield to peevish sorrow, lamenting and bemoaning death? Thou fool! if heretofore thou hast had pleasure of thy life and all delights have not mocked thy grasp and vanished away untasted like water poured into a leaking vessel, why dost thou not depart contented from the feast of life, and with heart at peace sleep the dreamless sleep? But if all thy pleasures have been squandered and lost, and life but offends thee, why seek to add thereto that which must itself be spent as ill and perish wholly unenjoyed? Is it not better to make an end of life and sorrow? I have no more pleasant inventions and devices for thee: all things are still the same. Though haply the years have not already wasted thy body, and thy limbs be not worn out and weary; yet all things abide the same; though thou shouldst outlive the generations of men; yea though thou shouldst never die."

The thing that hath been, it is that which shall be ; and that which is done is that which shall be done ; and there is no new thing under the sun.   But while for the Preacher death is simply a horror of gross darkness and the end of every man's desire, Lucretius rapturously welcomes it.

'*No more shalt thou have a glad welcome home and thy good wife and sweet children race to win the first kiss and touch thy heart with a silent content. No more mayest thou prosper in thy works and guard thine own. Hapless one in hapless wise,* men say, *one ruinous day has robbed thee of all the numerous gifts of life.* When they say this they do not add : *But now thou art not beset with the longing for these things any more.* Howbeit if they were to see this and put their thought into words, they would deliver themselves from great terror and travail of spirit. *Thou indeed for all time to come wilt be as now thou art, put to sleep by death, set free from all the heartache. But we wept for thee and would not be comforted when standing by we watched thee turn to ashes on the awful pyre, and time will not pluck the rooted sorrow from our hearts.* Then let us ask what great bitterness is found herein that it should make any man pine away in sorrow everlasting ? If it all comes to a sleep and a slumber at the last ? '

Just because this sentiment is so familiar to us in modern poetry we are perhaps apt to forget that it is not in the very least characteristic of antiquity. Ancient pessimism is for the most part simply the expression of that not unamiable melancholy which goes so naturally with the sensuous appreciation of life. Its cry is *Breuis est hic fructus homullis*—' Brief is the hour of enjoyment for pitiful Man '. It is a cry not for less of life but for more. To Lucretius it

appeared mere *Katzenjammer*: *aufer ab hinc lacrimas,
balatro*—'Away with you and your tears, you rascal!'

"Meurs, vieux lâche! il est trop tard!"

It is of course perfectly true that the lamentation
'Death is better than life' rises again and again in
ancient literature.   It only means that hearts were
broken in the old world as in the modern.   But who
save Lucretius preached the glad tidings of *annihi-
lation*?   To use a vivid phrase of George Fox's, he
'strikes at your life'.   He is more eloquent than
Spenser's Despayre; and it is evident that what
supplies his eloquence is his own passionate conviction.

It is this impression of intensity that seems to stay
with us longest.   The whole poem is instinct with a
spiritual excitement that reminds one of Shelley.   It
breaks out in sudden glories of almost flagrant colour
when the poet seems, in his own phrase, to mingle
coral with emeralds; it even penetrates into the vehe-
ment arguments which he pours forth in such profusion
and with such rapidity of utterance, like a man
desperately pleading.   Now this intensity should be
capable of explanation, and so should his strangely
modern pessimism.   I have indicated where I am
inclined to look for the explanation: in some experience of the kind which has given modern literature
so much to speak about.   At the cause indeed we can
only guess; but I think we know the disease, call it
what we like, *weltschmerz*, ennui, spiritual unrest. . . .
What I meant by adducing the case of Baudelaire was
to emphasize this; both are extreme men, though the

Roman is the larger spirit, and Baudelaire could never have designed and completed so important a structure as the *De Rerum Natura*. Both, to use sincerely the cheapened phrase, are 'tired of life'.

> *O Mort, vieux capitaine, il est temps! levons l'ancre!*
> *Ce pays nous ennuie, O Mort! Appareillons!*
> *Si le ciel et la mer sont noirs comme de l'encre,*
> *Nos cœurs que tu connais sont remplis de rayons!*

But Lucretius does not even hope for something new.

THE SPRINGS OF POETRY

THAT in us which is moved by poetry is evidently primordial, not recent or factitious. Suppose we knew in what manner of reaction to the universe the earliest poetry was made, would not also the nature of poetry as the expression of that reaction thereby become clearer? We should at least find a common denominator between the moods of the old and the new poets. The search for this has the advantage of dealing with the maker of the poem rather than immediately with the poem itself; which seems the right way of approaching the question.

By following it I have come to think that the emotion (if we may call it that) which is touched by poetry and expressed in it is a sense of the solidarity of our being with that of nature and our fellow men. What I mean by this it will be the business of the following pages to explain. Meanwhile I simply state the argument : which is that, the further back we trace it, the more conscious and realized is this feeling of the unity of man's life with that of the beasts and plants and stones, and the more nearly does poetry approach the nature of a spell which aims at evoking this senti-ment. And I conclude that poetry is still essentially a spell or charm (*carmen*) awakening or reawakening the sense that we are organic with the world.

Suppose us living in an earth-house of the type familiar to archaeologists. . . . We enter by a hole in the ground surrounded by a ring of stones, and so cunningly disposed that an enemy may pass close and never notice it. If he did, he would know that it leads to the underground chamber which is our storehouse and our living-room. During the winter we keep our live stock there too, our shaggy stunted cows and long-tailed sheep. Consequently, though we go quite naked or at best wearing a sheepskin or the like, it is never cold; on the contrary it is hot and steamy. Nevertheless we must always contrive to keep a fire burning, for, once out, it is so troublesome to rekindle. Moreover it is clearly a sacred and powerful animal or god, who bites you cruelly if you touch him. Yet the fire can be kindly too, and gives us light of nights, and may be used for the broiling of flesh (an innovation of doubtful morality), and warms the bones of our buried fathers. Hence we worship the Hearth. All winter we have been living chiefly upon milk and the grain and nuts we were careful to store in the earth-house during the autumn. Our only chance of flesh came when one of us ventured out on a hunting expedition, in spite of the snow which hides the trails. Our own cattle of course we would not eat; they are our brothers and sisters, and we are not cannibals. They belong to the family just as much as you or I, and the same blood runs in their veins.

If any of us died, we buried him under the hearth, that he might not complain of cold in his grave, for the dead are touchy and malicious. Not that they are really *dead*. They only go away somewhere else, leaving their bodies here. What they want is a new body, so that they may get born again and have another portion of life. There is no such thing as an absolutely new baby. It is only an ancestor beginning life over again.

We amused ourselves playing at cat's cradle with long grasses or the like, and telling each other interminable stories (which we helped to make clear by our actions) about our feats in the hunt and in single combat. But on the whole we are glad when the longer days come, and the snow disappears. We feel the Spring in our blood. We can now take our fill of fishing and hunting and fighting with the settlement on the other side of the hill. True, our weapons are not very serviceable. Some of us have only got clubs or stone balls; a few have flint knives. Such things are not of much use against a wild bull when he charges. We are indeed very helpless. On one side of us are the swamps, on the other the impenetrable forest, full of dangerous beasts. That is one reason why our roads always keep to the hills, where the trees stop, and it is possible to see where one is going. Many animals are both stronger and swifter than we. No doubt they are wiser as well. The birds at least certainly are, for they know what weather is coming. Our ancestors believed that many beasts were great magicians, and they were ready to worship them. But the chief danger is from ghosts, who are always on the watch to torment and kill us. What can we do except huddle closer to one another by the common fire, and pray for aid to our own dead or to our general mother the Earth, from whose bosom we sprang and in whose bosom also we shall lie at last?

That is an attempt to express some of the reflections

that moved darkly in the mind of the earth-house man. Do I think it at all successful? I do not; and the reason is that I have made him too imaginative. I cannot help it; but at least I have shown afresh the danger that besets all modern reconstructions of primitive thought. The imagination wants everything clear and separate, and so falls to the temptation of presenting the uncivilized man as possessed by a very few simple, crude, and extremely definite notions. Now this is all wrong. The savage has no clear ideas about anything. His mind is a mere *tohu-bohu* of vague and contradictory presumptions. He is (against the popular view) profoundly unimaginative. Or perhaps it were more exact to say that his imagination is at the mercy of a number of conventions, which to us are quite irrational and even unmeaning. It is these conventions we have to study if we propose to understand the savage. The conclusion is paradoxical, but we are dealing with a paradoxical animal. That certain instincts of human nature are fundamental and permanent, I not only admit but shall be forced to assume. But the doctrine that 'human nature is always the same' is only true if we reduce the word 'same' to so impoverished a content that it makes the sentence apter to mislead than to guide. It has done a deal of mischief already.

For instance, we hold that man is distinguished from the beasts by his possession of self-consciousness. But what does the savage say? He says that his soul is not his own. He does not think for himself; the group thinks for him. By the 'group' I here mean the human members of a primitive community. For such a community, as I shall have to repeat, is not simply an association of human beings, but embraces everything, animate and inanimate, in which its men and women are vitally interested. The metaphor surviving in words like Corporation and Body Politic was once held to be no metaphor at all. Men and herds, the earth and its fruits, were within the limits of the 'tribe' one body and one blood and one soul. Australian peoples explain that they and their possessions are "All-one-flesh." The sentiment fades in intensity as culture progresses; but it is one of the roots of culture. Poetry, I think, has grown out of it.

Let me begin at what may seem the wrong end; let me take so typically modern a poet as Wordsworth. Wordsworth's heart 'leaps up' when he beholds 'a rainbow in the sky', and 'dances with the daffodils', his days being 'bound each to each by natural piety', which is also a kind of filial piety towards the Mother who gives her child, Man, of her own life and dim-stirring memories.   He says of his choice of subjects :—
'Humble and rustic life was generally chosen, because, in that condition, the essential passions of the heart find a better soil in which they can attain their maturity, are less under restraint, and speak a plainer and more emphatic language; because in that condition of life our elementary feelings co-exist in a state of greater simplicity, and, consequently, may be more accurately contemplated, and more forcibly communicated; because the manners of rural life germinate from those elementary feelings, and, from the necessary character of rural occupations, are more easily comprehended, and are more durable; and, lastly, because in that condition the passions of men are incorporated with the beautiful and

permanent forms of nature.' This, however, is a somewhat prosaic account of the matter. And we may ask, what are 'the essential passions of the heart', by what processes do they become 'incorporated with the beautiful and permanent forms of nature'?

His poetry gives us the answer. He says in the *Prelude*:

> *I remember when the changeful earth*
> *And twice five summers on my mind had stamped*
> *The faces of the moving year, even then*
> *I held unconscious intercourse with beauty*
> *Old as creation, drinking in a pure*
> *Organic pleasure from the silver wreaths*
> *Of curling mist, or from the level plain*
> *Of waters coloured by impending clouds.*

He speaks of himself as standing

> *Beneath some rock, listening to notes that are*
> *The ghostly language of the ancient earth,*
> *Or make their dim abode in distant winds.*
> *Thence did I drink the visionary power;*
> *And deem not profitless those fleeting moods*
> *Of shadowy exultation: not for this,*
> *That they are kindred to our purer mind*
> *And intellectual life; but that the soul,*
> *Remembering how she felt, but what she felt*
> *Remembering not, retains an obscure sense*
> *Of possible sublimity.*

And in the most famous of his poems he brings in this theory of a previous existence to account for precisely such subconscious emotions as he might, if he were living now, be content to explain by the workings of a long race-memory.

> *Though nothing can bring back the hour*
> *Of splendour in the grass, of glory in the flower;*

We will grieve not, rather find
Strength in what remains behind;
In the primal sympathy
Which having been must ever be.

He is again appealing to this 'primal sympathy' when in the *Excursion* he asks

Has not the soul, the being of your life,
Received a shock of awful consciousness,
In some calm season, when these lofty rocks
At night's approach bring down the unclouded sky,
To rest upon their circumambient walls?

So Wordsworth's doctrine only needs a little restatement, a greater emphasis on the inherited character of man's primal sympathy with nature, to agree with the impression one gets from a study of the anthropological evidence.   When he is making poetry without reference to any theory, we come (as often happens with the poets) closer to his secret.

My horse moved on; hoof after hoof
He raised, and never stopped:
When down behind the cottage-roof,
At once, the bright moon dropped.

What fond and wayward thoughts will slide
Into a Lover's head!
"O mercy!" to myself I cried,
"If Lucy should be dead!"

Is not this association of the setting of the moon with the death of the beloved as old as the heart of man? Do we not feel behind it the emotions which created the belief that the destinies of men hung on the moon and stars?

Wordsworth is full of lines like these :—

> *The Rock, like something starting from a sleep,*
> *Took up the Lady's voice, and laughed again;*
> *That ancient Woman seated on Helm-crag*
> *Was ready with her cavern; Hammer-scar,*
> *And the tall Steep of Silver-how, sent forth*
> *A noise of laughter; southern Loughrigg heard,*
> *And Fairfield answered with a mountain tone;*
> *Helvellyn far into the clear blue sky*
> *Carried the Lady's voice,—old Skiddaw blew*
> *His speaking-trumpet;—back out of the clouds*
> *Of Glaramara southward came the voice;*
> *And Kirkstone tossed it from his misty head.*
> *—Now whether . . . this were in simple truth*
> *A work accomplished by the brotherhood*
> *Of ancient mountains, or my ear was touched*
> *With dreams and visionary impulses*
> *To me alone imparted, sure I am*
> *That there was a loud uproar in the hills.*

One feels behind those lines, again, the emotions that have formed mythologies.   And behind these, upon the four yewtrees of Borrowdale :

> *Huge trunks! and each particular trunk a growth*
> *Of intertwisted fibres serpentine*
> *Up-coiling, and inveterately convolved;*
> *Nor uninformed with Phantasy, and looks*
> *That threaten the profane;—a pillared shade*

with what follows to the fine last line

> *Murmuring from Glaramara's inmost caves.*

And behind these :

> *A trouble, not of clouds, or weeping rain,*
> *Nor of the setting sun's pathetic light*

> *Engendered, hangs o'er Eildon's triple height :*
> *Spirits of Power, assembled there, complain*
> *For kindred Power departing from their sight;*
> *While Tweed, best pleased in chanting a blithe strain,*
> *Saddens his voice again, and yet again.*

He says in the *Prelude*, speaking of his childhood,

> *I was alone,*
> *And seemed to be a trouble to the peace*
> *That dwelt among them.*

That is, among the moon and stars.

> *Sometimes it befel*
> *In these night wanderings, that a strong desire*
> *O'erpowered my better reason, and the bird*
> *Which was the captive of another's toil*
> *Became my prey ; and when the deed was done*
> *I heard among the solitary hills*
> *Low breathings coming after me, and sounds*
> *Of undistinguishable motion, steps*
> *Almost as silent as the turf they trod.*

And again, at the end of a passage which excellently illustrates the whole Wordsworthian attitude to nature, he speaks of

> *Huge and mighty forms, that do not live*
> *Like living men, moved slowly through the mind*
> *By day, and were a trouble to my dreams.*

If this were an experience confined to Wordsworth, it would merely stir our curiosity, it would not reawaken in us ancestral terrors of That which is always waiting for us in lonely places. Here is a similar passage :

> *A casual glance had shown them, and I fled,*
> *Faltering and faint, and ignorant of the road:*
> *Then, reascending the bare common, saw*
> *A naked pool that lay beneath the hills,*
> *The beacon on the summit, and, more near,*
> *A girl, who bore a pitcher on her head*
> *And seemed with difficult steps to force her way*
> *Against the blowing wind. It was, in truth,*
> *An ordinary sight; but I should need*
> *Colours and words that are unknown to man,*
> *To paint the visionary dreariness*
> *Which, while I looked all round for my lost guide,*
> *Invested moorland waste, and naked pool,*
> *The beacon crowning the lone eminence,*
> *The female and her garments vexed and tossed*
> *By the strong wind.*

If you can enter into the feeling of that passage, without letting yourself be too much disturbed by 'the female', you will get deep into Wordsworth's mind.

He at last definitely recognizes the primal sympathy as inherited. In the sonnet upon *The Monument commonly called Long Meg and her Daughters, near the River Eden* he says:

> *A weight of awe, not easy to be borne,*
> *Fell suddenly upon my Spirit—cast*
> *From the dread bosom of the unknown past,*
> *When first I saw that family forlorn;*

he recognizes it in

> *Only perchance some melancholy Stream*
> *And some indignant Hills old names preserve;*

above all in the lines which express the soul of all poetry :

Will no one tell me what she sings ?—
Perhaps the plaintive numbers flow
For old, unhappy, far-off things,
And battles long ago :
Or is it some more humble lay,
Familiar matter of to-day ?
Some natural sorrow, loss, or pain,
That has been, and may be again?

Poetry links the experience of to-day with the total experience of humanity; its substance is 'what has been and may be again'.

It may seem strange, but it is true, that Wordsworth's attitude to nature is just the attitude of the savage. The sole difference is that Wordsworth can render it in words—words that are possibly too precise for what is so irrational and indeterminate. The savage is exactly a creature moving about in worlds not realized, and he too believes 'there is a Spirit in the woods' and that when their leaves tremble in the sunshine 'there was pleasure there'. The sole difference is indeed an excessively important one. It is what makes Wordsworth a poet. But the emotional attitude or *diathesis*, which Wordsworth is a poet because he can interpret and the savage none because he cannot, is in both fundamentally the same.

Poetry is an art and therefore demands an effort of detachment for its making. This is just what the savage least of all people can exert. He gets absorbed in the object of his contemplation to that degree that he loses all sense of distinction between it and himself. It is not poetry to repeat (as a savage will) over and over again "I am an Eagle Hawk", if you believe it. It is a mere statement of fact, or what you conceive to be fact. You are saying it, not because your imagination is touched, but because you have not imagination enough to see that you are nothing of the kind. When you have ceased to believe that you are in fact an eagle hawk, then indeed the chant is on the way to become poetry. It is reawakening an emotion remembered in tranquillity, which is Wordsworth's definition of poetry, and the best yet offered.

The least sophisticated poem which may fairly be called great is perhaps the *Kalevala*. You can see in it the stuff out of which poetry is made. The characters in the *Kalevala* are mostly magicians who can turn themselves into any shape they please. Miracles are always happening. You are pretty sure of getting an answer from a bird or a tree, if you question it in the right way. You think of our Fairy Tales, of Aesop's fables, of Greek and Celtic mythology. These things preserve the *diathesis* of ancient men.

The *Kalevala* is made up of very old lays. But take a modern instance, Shelley's *Hymn of Pan*. The reader will not get much from it unless he can recapture the mood of Pan, who *saw* a girl turn into a reed. Something stirs in us—the conviction we might have thought killed by centuries of education, that in this wonderful world of ours anything may happen. The poet plays on this latent conviction, 'makes', as Shelley himself expresses it, 'the common as if it were not common'. Consider the story of Syrinx from this point of view. Pan was the god of the Arcadian goatherds. He is represented as half a man and half a goat. A type of this sort expresses the solidarity of the community which projects it. Pan is the projection of countless rituals, where the men of the tribe demonstrated their kinship with the goats by dressing up as goats. And because they played upon pipes cut from the syrinx-reed, he must play on a similar pipe. But his pipe (they would argue) is not like ours, altogether; it is a god's and magical; it is alive. And it has a shrill treble voice like a girl. It *is* a girl. If you go down to the lake-side you will see a great reed shrinking from the wind like a frightened girl. . . . The story might grow up in that way. At least we may be sure that at every step in its growth the imaginations of the herdsmen were bound by the actual circumstances of their lives. The imagination of the poet is not so bound. It can travel. It lets him into other people's houses. This he does by what is called 'imaginative sympathy'. But what is that except a sense of the tribal solidarity, with this difference, that the sense is now more reflective, and the 'tribe' now the whole race and the whole of nature? You cannot understand another man's feelings unless by force of sympathy you do for the moment become the other man.

Now the savage is unable to conceive any mode of living widely different from his own. He believes that the dead, the beasts and the birds have their tribes and assemblies and dances like himself. Anthropologists have observed that savages do not believe it possible for a man to die by natural causes. No one dies, he is killed. Life is everywhere, in everything. They cannot understand why an oak or a rock should not have life like a man. Why should it not speak? Why should it not be your father? People in Hesiod's time thought you might be born of an oak or a rock.

All this is because the natural man cannot help attributing himself to everything he sees. Pascal says 'Perhaps nature is a first custom, just as custom is a second nature'. Yet it is certain that from the very first man must have had latent somewhere in him the impulse to break the bonds of habit and custom. He is the only iconoclastic animal. He has had to buy his success with infinite suffering; but his suffering has taught him sympathy, or rather developed the germ of imaginative sympathy which was in him at the beginning. Mr. Belloc says in one of his books:

'There are primal things which move us. Fire has the character of a free companion that has travelled with us from the first exile; only to see a fire, whether he need it or no, comforts every man. Again, to hear two voices outside at night after a silence, even in crowded cities, transforms the mind. A Roof also, large and mothering, satisfies us here in the north much more than modern necessity can explain; so we built in beginning: the only way to carry off our rains and to bear the weight of our winter snows. A Tower far off arrests a man's eye always; it is more than a break in the sky-line; it is an enemy's watch or the rallying of a defence to whose aid we are summoned. Nor are these emotions a memory or a reversion only as one crude theory might pretend; we craved these things—the camp, the refuge, the sentinels in the dark, the hearth—before we made them; they are part of our human manner, and when this civilization has perished they will reappear.'

So Mr. Yeats cries to the *Everlasting Voices*:

> *Have you not heard that our hearts are old,*
> *That you call in birds, in wind on the hill,*
> *In shaken boughs, in tide on the shore?*

Poetry stirs the inherited and accumulated memories,

and under the memories the instincts that make us cherish them, of all the generations. It gives us the sense of boundless horizons and incalculable emotions. When, for instance, Wordsworth says :

> *The sounding cataract*
> *Haunted me like a passion,*

do not the words awaken an obscure and slumbering recollection of times when we lived within hearing of the cataract, and were appalled and fascinated by it, and worshipped it ? I am not leaving out aesthetic considerations. I am trying to find why the words are beautiful. For we do not admire beauty abstractly, it must touch some responding chord in us, it must move us more than we can explain. No doubt in some way poetry does transform experience—the experience of the race stored up in us. But to transform it, it must deal with it.

Almost any descriptive line in Homer will give an instance.

> ἦμος δ᾽ἠριγένεια φάνη ῥοδοδάκτυλος Ἠώς
> '*When, early born, rose-fingered Dawn shone out*',

or

> ἠερίη δ᾽ἀνέβη μέγαν Οὐρανὸν Οὔλυμπόν τε
> '*Early in the morning she ascended huge Heaven and Olympus*',

or

> ὅθι τ᾽ Ἠοῦς ἠριγενείης
> οἰκία καὶ χοροί εἰσι καὶ ἀντολὰι Ἠελίοιο
> '*Where Dawn's child the Morning has her chambers and her dancing-places, and the Sun his uprisings*'.

Add Dante's

> *Dolce color d'oriental zaffiro;*

Shakespeare's

> *Jocund day*
> *Stands tiptoe on the misty mountain top*

and

> *But look where Morn with russet mantle clad*
> *Walks o'er the dew of that high eastern hill.*

Add Tennyson's

> *God made himself an awful rose of dawn;*

and Morris' *Summer Dawn*:

> *Pray but one prayer for me 'twixt thy closed lips. . . .*

Lines like these gather up the colour and solemnity of all the dawns since man came on the earth.

Hear the poets again upon night: Sappho with her

> δέδυκε μὲν ἀ σέλαννα
> καὶ Πληίαδες, μέσαι δὲ
> νύκτες, παρὰ δ'ἔρχετ' ὤρα,
> ἔγω δὲ μόνα κατεύδω.

'*The moon has set, and the Pleiads. Midnight; and the hour is passing; and I am lying alone*';

Virgil with his

> *Quale per incertam lunam sub luce maligna*
> *Est iter in siluis.*

'*As one walketh in wild places in feeble moonshine and a ghastly glimmer*'.

There is Tennyson's line

In the dead, unhappy night, and when the rain is on the roof;

and Whitman's wonderful phrase

> *The huge and thoughtful night.*

These words—and so many more that one might quote —contain the sanctity of the ancient darkness. They are haunted words, symbols, troubling us with ancestral terrors of the night.

Again, the sea has been a great inspiration. There is a wonderful sea-feeling all through Greek poetry, notably in the *Odyssey*.

> Αἰαίην δ'ἐς νῆσον ἀφικόμεθ' · ἔνθα δ'ἔναιεν
> Κίρκη ἐυπλόκαμος, δεινὴ θεὸς αὐδήεσσα,
> αὐτοκασιγνήτη ὀλοόφρονος Αἰήταο.

'*We came to the Aeaean Isle. There lived Circe of the beautiful hair, an awful goddess with human words, and sister of the weird Aeetes.*'

Compare

> *We were the first that ever burst*
> *Into that silent sea.—*

and

> *Voyaging through strange seas of thought alone.*

As we read we recover the excitement of the first navigators. And again, what Wordsworth calls 'of the old sea some reverential fear' stirs in us when we read

> *Placed far amid the melancholy main*

or

> *The moving waters at their priest-like task*
> *Of pure ablution round earth's human shores*

or Lucretius'

placidi pellacia ponti

or the great

πovτίων τε κυμάτων
ἀνήριθμον γέλασμα
'*the multitudinous laughter of the sea.*'

Of lonely places and the sentiment of the wild. Aeschylus says :

χθονὸς μὲν ἐς τηλουρὸν ἥκομεν πέδον,
Σκύθην ἐς οἶμον, ἄβατον εἰς ἐρημίαν.
'*We have come to a far-off floor of the world, the Scythian trail, the untrodden wilderness*'.

Per loca pastorum deserta atque otia dia
'*Among the quiet, dreamy places, where none but the shepherds come*'.

Euripides had this line in his lost *Ino* :

κοίλοις ἐν ἄντροις ἄλυχνος, ὥστε θὴρ μόνος
'*Lightless in hollow caves, like a solitary beast.*'

Odysseus in the tenth book of the *Odyssey* describes how in his loneliness he saw a great sight—'a tall high-antlered stag right on my tracks' :

ὃ μὲν ποταμόνδε κατήιεν ἐκ νομοῦ ὕλης
πιόμενος · δὴ γάρ μιν ἔχεν μένος ἠελίοιο.
'*He was coming down from the rough pasture-land to drink in the river, for he felt the rage of the sun*'.

Itur in antiquam siluam, stabula alta ferarum,

says Virgil :

'*They enter an old deep wood, where wild things laired*'.

This way of speaking makes the most civilized of us suddenly discontented with the life of cities. Two ancient poets seem to me to command it especially : Euripides in the *Bacchae* and Lucretius. And of course Homer :—

'*Very strong were they, and with the strongest they fought, even with the Beast-men that wonned in the mountain-caves, and wrought wild slaughter among them*'.

We were all in that fight, one side or the other. The Plains have always had to defend themselves from the Hills.

I add, as they occur to me, lines of a somewhat more subtle appeal :

Child Rolana to the dark tower came.—

Lady of the mere
Sole-sitting by the shores of old Romance—

Magic casements opening on the foam
Of perilous seas in faery lands forlorn—

Dieu! que le son du cor est triste au fond des bois!

When we listen to such words our heart remembers the time when man really seemed to himself to move among things enchanted. When we say their effect is 'magical' we speak truer than we know ; they reveal a world other than the world we tread on.

Yes, there is magic in them. This can be shown in a manner historically. For it is certain that poetry in its origins was mixed up with other arts (in *their* rudimentary state), and notably with music and dancing; and that all was done with magical intent. Undoubtedly the oldest of the arts is dancing. To say this is not to imply that the dance was ever unaccompanied by rhythmical noises of some kind. The silent dances you sometimes find among savages may be imitations of the silent dances of certain birds and animals. What I mean is that dancing is an elaborate art among peoples so rude that they have no other art at all. The reason is that for such folks dancing is altogether the most solemn and vital business of their lives. It is not done simply for the pleasure of it (though it is pleasurable), but in deadly earnest and for the most important reasons: namely, to increase the tribe and its sources of food. In a very actual and even tragic sense the dancers dance for their living.— And this is magic.

Magic is an operation which presumes on the existence of a special bond of sympathy between the magician and the person or thing on which he is working. When a sailor whistles for a wind (if sailors do) he must vaguely believe in some kind of sympathetic connexion between himself and the wind. If an Australian Blackfellow disguises himself as an emu and carefully imitates its deportment, he conceives that by this behaviour he is somehow causing the emus to increase and multiply? How, unless there is some mystic bond between them? A traveller, who has seen it, has a description of the Grizzly Bear dance of the North American Indians. The drummers assemble and chant *I begin to grow restless in the spring*—here, you see, is poetry coming in, as an accompaniment of the dance—and they represent the bear making ready to leave his winter den.   Then, as Mr. McClintock saw the thing, Lone Chief drew his robe about him and arose to dance, imitating the bear going from his lair, and chanting :

> *I take my robe,*
> *My robe is sacred,*
> *I wander in the summer.*

Lone Chief with his hands imitated a bear holding up its paws, and placing his feet together, he moved backward and forward with short jumps, making the lumbering movements that a bear makes, running, breathing heavily, and pretending to dig and turn over stones for insects.   This is not an eccentric but a typical primitive dance.   Most imitate the movements of animals.   The underlying sentiment is what we set out by observing.   The tribesman thinks that the animals he tames or hunts, the plants he eats, the spirits he worships, are all members of one great family. The birds and beasts and blossoms are (so to speak) our elder brothers and know a good deal more than we, especially about the weather.   You will say, we have got over all that.   Yes, we have driven it down into our subconsciousness.   But it is still there.   It must be there, because it was for ages on ages the most potent conviction of the human mind.   It inspires in a half conscious way parts of Hesiod, parts of the *Song of Songs*, the *Kalevala*, other things.   St. Francis preached to the birds and fishes, and made friends with a wolf. . . . Read any descriptive poetry and see how little it moves you until it strikes the mysterious note that merges your soul in nature's.

The description of poetry as a medium or conductor

between the experience of the individual and the total experience of the race is perhaps only a translation into concrete terms of the definition suggested by metaphysicians when they say that the business of poetry is to reveal the universal in the particular. It only remains to ask, how does it apply to rhythm—a vital element in poetry? Well, rhythm is the soul of dancing. It has an intoxicating effect; I mean, it excites one part of our nature and dulls another. Just as suggestible people may be hypnotized by a monotonous sound, we may suppose that the regular beat of metrical rhythm lulls the waking consciousness into a partial sleep, thus allowing the subconscious part of our minds to have its chance. The first poetry was a spell to help out the magic of the dance; the first poets were magicians; and the magician knows the entrancing influence of rhythm. What gives it this power is much of a mystery. All we know is: χορεύει ὁ κόσμος, the Universe treads a measure, and our very blood is rhythmical. Not poetry nor the dance created rhythm; rather the instinct for rhythm created them.—And that is perhaps all that can be said profitably about rhythm.

If I have illustrated my argument from the poetry of nature, it is because anyone can illustrate it for himself from that kind of poetry (making up nine-tenths of the whole) which appeals directly from man to man.

SOME THOUGHTS ON TRANSLATION

ANYONE may see that translation from the ancient classics is difficult, we do it so badly. This is not for want of trying. It has always been a favourite English amusement, taken with the proper seriousness. The mere mass of such translation is enormous ; it has attracted excellent brains ; occasionally it has attracted genius. Yet if one were condemned to read it all, or even a large part of it (for more would hardly be practicable), I think one might prefer hanging. It is a great pity. Everybody cannot learn Latin and Greek, and there is perhaps no learning about which one can say with greater truth that a little of it is dangerous. The plain man, feeling this, looks to the trained scholar for something that will suggest to him the charm and significance residing in ancient literature. Does he get it ? The scholar either declines to translate on the ground that all translation is an outrage upon the original, or (too often) translates for other scholars in a curious traditional diction, which may have the most admirable exegetic virtues, but is scarcely to be called the English language. One reason for the eagerness with which Professor Gilbert Murray's translations of the *Hippolytus* and the *Bacchae* were welcomed by the public was the contrast they made with the colourless and unidiomatic language we had come to think of as the native speech

15

of the gods. We had been told, and had dutifully believed it, that Euripides was a poet. But here was the proof of it. Our surprise was eloquent.

That the translator must possess certain special qualifications for his task goes without saying, and that, if he lack even one of these, he will fail. It is indeed a very unusual combination of qualities he requires. Yet we find it in Fitzgerald's *Omar*, in Rossetti's *Early Italian Poets*, in Swinburne's and Mr. John Payne's translations from Villon. The number of people who can read old Persian or medieval Italian or medieval French is very much smaller in this country than the numbers who can read Latin and Greek ; and if we were to count the heads of translators, I feel sure the disproportion would be greater still. The classical scholars (it would seem) have not produced their fair share of successful versions. We cannot say that it is because the spirit of the classics is more alien to the modern spirit than is Cavalcanti's or Villon's. We find Euripides and Theocritus, Catullus and Horace, I will not say more sympathetic than Villon, but more at one with us in their aesthetic and intellectual standards—in a word more modern. It looks paradoxical, but it is now an accepted paradox. Well, this being so, why do we not translate the ancient poets on the whole so well ? As it happens, Euripides and Theocritus have been exceptionally fortunate in their translators. But think of the versions—how many ?—of Catullus and Horace. What is one to say of them ? In this way or in that, some are really so good. Yet, for a reason, it is the comparative goodness of these which appears to afflict us most with a sense of their desolating futility as a whole. Which leads us back to the proposition that it must be very hard to translate the classics.

It is the consciousness of this which may be responsible for the extravagant amount of theory which has been aired by translators. I hope it is no very cynical asperity to say Beware of the translator with a theory. There is only one right way of translating (as Aristotle would say), and an infinite number of wrong ways. When you begin to reflect at cross roads you are lost. Even if your theory be right, you may fail in practice. Or again a man may translate wonderfully, and give a wrong explanation of his success. It is fundamentally, though not entirely, a matter of genius and temperament. Dryden, himself an admirable translator, speaks on the subject with an engaging candour.

'Methinks, I come like a malefactor, to make a speech upon the gallows, and to warn all other poets, by my sad example, from the sacrilege of translating Virgil."

That is very disarming. But it is of course a counsel of despair. If however you must translate poetry, Dryden was at least ready with a piece of negative advice: Do not attempt to be literal! 'It is almost impossible', he says, 'to translate verbally, and well, at the same time.'

This was the general view about Dryden's time. Sir John Denham in the Preface to his *Destruction of Troy* which was 'an Essay on the second book of Virgil's Aeneis' has this remark :

'It is not his'—that is, the translator's—'business alone to translate language into language, but poesy into poesy; and poesy is of so subtile a spirit, that in the pouring out of one language into another, it will all evaporate ; and if a new spirit be not added in the transfusion, there will remain nothing but a *caput mortuum*, there being certain graces and happinesses peculiar to every language, which give life and energy to the words ; and whosoever offers at verbal translation, shall have the misfortune of that young traveller, who lost his own language abroad, and brought home no other instead of it.'

That is brilliantly put, and indeed seems almost unanswerable. Cowley in the Preface to his translations from Pindar takes the same view in words that are almost famous.

'If a man should undertake to translate Pindar, word for word, it would be thought that one madman had translated another ; as may appear, when he that understands not the original, reads the verbal traduction of him into Latin prose, than which nothing seems more raving.'

That Cowley is very right jumps to the eyes when you read a 'verbal traduction' of Pindar even into English prose. I will here set down what I have found on opening such a translation. The passage comes in the second *Olympian* :—

'There are many swift darts under my elbow, within my quiver, which have a voice for those with understanding, but to the crowd they need interpreters. He is gifted with genius who knoweth much by natural talent, but those who have learnt, boisterous in gabbling, like daws, clamour in fruitless fashion against the divine bird of Zeus.

'Keep now the bow on the mark ; come, my spirit, whom do we strike at, sending again shafts of good report from a benevolent spirit ? At Agragas verily stretching my bow, I will utter an oath-bound word from a sincere soul, viz. that even for a hundred years that city has brought forth no other hero more beneficent in heart to his friends, or more ungrudging in hand, than Theron.

'But envy loves to attack praise, not encountering it fairly, but from senseless men, which loves to babble and to obscure the noble deeds of the good. Since the sand escapes numbering, as to our hero, what pleasures he has given to others, who can tell?'

What does it all mean? Really, Cowley's is the only comment one can make: it is exactly as if one madman had translated another. Nor, as one turns over the leaves of the book, does one get any respite from absurdity. There are sentences like this:

'I fancy I have upon my tongue a sharp-sounding whetstone,[b] which *fancy* creeps over me willing amongst sweet-flowing song.'

[b] v. 82: lit.—was ever translator so conscientious? —'lit. I have the fancy, or feeling, on my tongue of a sharp-sounding whetstone.'

And what does this mean?

'And in a brief song will I make innumerable *victories to shine* conspicuous, and there shall accompany me the true, sweet-tongued voice, bound by oath, heard sixty times from both spots, of the fortunate herald.'

One may discover the meaning by applying to the Greek. But the business of a translator is to translate. As regards this version of Pindar, it is no worse than others composed on the same principle. My readers who have had the inestimable advantage of a classical education will remember them. It was Dr. Johnson who said they would survive as the clandestine refuge of schoolboys.

Verbal translation of poetry into poetry is an unrealizable dream, and indeed shows a rather foolish ambition in the translator who attempts it. Where the original is extremely simple in style, it may be possible for someone with a fine sense of literature to produce a version which will be nearly literal, and still be good English. Andrew Lang's translations of Homer and Theocritus are like that. But they are in prose, and that is not what we want; we want poetry rendered into poetry. It cannot be done very simply. Poetry is not produced by a combination of meanings only, but as well by a combination of sounds and rhythms and various other elements, and it cannot be reproduced except in that way. It will sometimes happen that the word you find to render a word in the original will have not only the same meaning but an equal poetical value. But the difficulty increases with a phrase—I mean, if you are translating quite literally—and becomes absolute with a sentence. Dryden saw this clearly, as he could not fail to see it. But he went to the other extreme. If not the inventor, he was (until Pope arrived with his *Homer*) the most influential practitioner of what one might call the compensation theory of translation. According to this, the translator is to make up for the deficiencies of his version when he must render the more inimitable parts of his author by adding, whenever an opportunity offers, new 'beauties' of his own. When the translator has a literary faculty like Dryden's, the result will be as good as the *Virgil*. But it will not be a translation. The *Virgil* is not a translation; it is a paraphrase. How the method

works in less competent hands may be seen in what I
will now quote—a very few lines will be enough—from
a translation into verse of that very ode of which a part
has already been given translated into literal prose.
The author was a 'Mr. Abraham Moore', and his
version is recommended to the reader as 'distinguished
for poetry, scholarship, and taste'.

> *Heed not thou their envious tongue,*
> *Straight to the mark advance thy bow;*
> *Whither, brave spirit, shall thy song*
> *Throw the shaft of glory now?*
> *Lo it flies, by Justice sent,*
> *Full at famous Agrigent;*
> *While truth inspires me thus to swear,*
> *That Time shall waste his hundredth year*
> *Ere race or realm a King shall raise,*
> *Whose liberal heart, whose loaded hand*
> *Shall paragon with Theron's praise,*
> *Or strew, like his, its blessings through the land.*

On the whole one prefers the literal version. It is at
least innocent of such a diction. Yet our complacency
may be disturbed when we reflect that this metrical
version undoubtedly gave pleasure to many people in
the age when public taste affected this particular kind
of *cliché*. (It prefers a different kind now). Also the
Advertisement says that, as it is 'among the rarest and
most expensive volumes of our modern literature, the
literary public will have reason to be satisfied with its
reproduction on such advantageous terms'. I suppose
there is no writing perishes so quickly as verse-
translations, unless they are done supremely well. But
I think this is quite right.

Even if the 'added beauties' should be a fair
compensation, this is not the right way to translate. It

is not translation at all, for it does not give us what a translation promises, which is the original, the whole original, and nothing but that.   We have all laughed at

Set Bacchus from his glassy prison free,
And strip white Ceres of her nut-brown coat

for Homer's 'Open the bottle and cut the bread'. Rossetti in the Preface to his *Early Italian Poets* says very well and truly :

'The task of the translator (and with all humility be it spoken) is one of some self-denial.   Often he would avail himself of any special grace of his own idiom and epoch, if only his will belonged to him : often would some cadence serve him but for his author's structure— some structure but for his author's cadence : often the beautiful turn of a stanza must be weakened to adopt some rhyme which will tally, and he sees the poet revelling in abundance of language where himself is scantily supplied.   Now he would slight the matter for the music, and now the music for the matter ; but no,— he must deal to each alike.   Sometimes too a flaw in the work galls him, and he would fain remove it, doing for the poet that which his age denied him ; but no,—it is not in the bond.   His path is like that of Aladdin through the enchanted vaults : many are the precious fruits and flowers which he must pass by unheeded in search for the lamp alone ; happy if at last, when brought to light, it does not prove that his old lamp has been exchanged for a new one,—glittering indeed to the eye, but scarcely of the same virtue nor with the same genius at its summons.'

Verse translation cannot be literal ; yet it must be faithful ; above all—for this is the very soul of its faithfulness—it must be poetical. Rossetti speaks such golden sense on this matter, that I must be allowed to quote again from his Preface.

' The life-blood of rhymed translation is this—that a good poem shall not be turned into a bad one. The only true motive for putting poetry into a fresh language must be to endow a fresh nation, as far as possible, with one more possession of beauty. Poetry not being an exact science, literality of rendering is altogether secondary to this chief aim. I say *literality*, —not fidelity, which is by no means the same thing. When literality can be combined with what is thus the primary condition of success, the translator is fortunate, and must strive his utmost to unite them ; when such object can only be attained by paraphrase, that is his only path.'

By ' paraphrase ' Rossetti means something quite different from Dryden, to whom it means pretty much what we call ' padding '—done, it must be admitted, as only Dryden could do it. Rossetti does not propose to add anything to the sense of his author. Only sometimes, he means, it cannot be captured by direct assault, and the translator has to attempt a turning movement.

He who translates out of the Latin and Greek is perpetually confronted by this obstacle, and this it is which makes his task so hard. It is not any difficulty of interpretation. I say this because people sometimes talk as if it were. The true business of the translator is not to get at the sense of his author (which he is assumed to know already), but to convey it to others. Grasping the sense is all preliminary work, as the deciphering of documents is for the historian. His proper work is finding the right English words to render the Latin or Greek. And the reason why that is so peculiarly difficult is as we have seen. The genius of the ancient languages differs profoundly from the genius of our own. The number and the nature of their differences cannot be discussed, even cursorily, here. But one may touch on one or two of the most important.

In the first place, then, I would say that modern English poetry differs from Latin and Greek (but especially from Greek) in the use of *colour*. We use it not only much more abundantly, but over a much wider range of shades and *nuances*, for Greek tints were few and definite. In this, as in every other generalization of the kind, exceptions are to be taken. There is in some Greek poets, as for instance Pindar and Theocritus, colour which is even lavish. But even in Pindar it is scarcely used for its own sake or deliberately sought after, except in so far as the traditional style of the choral lyric demands it; simply he had, unusually for a Greek, a naturally pictorial imagination. He is exceptional. Theocritus on the other hand was an Alexandrine, working on a very definite conception of what poetry can accomplish, among other things in the way of colour; and all these vignettes of his are very carefully studied. Yet it would not be true to say of any Idyll that it exists solely for the sake of the descriptions to be found in it, although one might say this of, for instance, the *Palace of Art*, which is not improved by its moral; and in any case Theocritus is of the Decadence. If we take the great central period of Greek poetry, Sophocles, who to many critics seems typically representative, is almost destitute of colour. And what strikes one in the Greeks as a whole is the extraordinary value they find in form and outline, and their comparative carelessness of everything else. This is partly instinctive in them, but it is also partly deliberate, because the absence or simplicity of background and accessories fixes the attention on the form so disengaged. And what a modern feels as an almost miserable parsimony of colour has the same effect. To put it quite simply, the Greeks were more interested in the shapes than in the colours of things. In Romantic poetry the opposite interest is found.

Everyone feels that this is so, and there is no need to illustrate or to elaborate the point. An extreme severity and purity of line, a sparing use of colour and ornament, are essential in the classical style. The importance of design, of construction, of clean outlines is everywhere felt. It is felt even in the choral style with its heaped richness of epithet and brusque transitions; the ordering of a Pindaric ode is like a plan of battle. This manner of the Greeks has been constantly imitated; with most assiduity, and perhaps with most success, in the eighteenth century (though then in a derivative way, through the Latin writers). Hence, even if we feel that its secret has never been wholly recaptured, everybody, whether he knows Greek or not, has a fair idea of what the classical style is like. How different it is from the modern manner is plain the moment you begin to read or remember any number of lines in a Romantic poem. Contrast the cry of Cassandra in Aeschylus:

Ah, ah, for the fate of the clear-voiced nightingale! For her the gods folded in a winged body, and a sweet life: but for me abides rending with a two-edged spear.

with Keats's ode. Or think of Swinburne's paraphrase
of Sappho's few, simple, almost colourless words into
Anactoria. Or reverse the process and try to imagine
—but it is impossible—a Greek *Paradise Lost* or *Eve of
St. Agnes* or *Lotos Eaters* or *Love in the Valley*. Such
colour would have seemed to an ancient critic a kind of
debauchery, our love of it merely barbaric.

A second distinguishing mark of English poetry is
its greater *realism*. The word is much misused and
overused, and I employ it here with some hesitation.
Perhaps it ought not to be applied to style at all. It is
not the style of a writer that is realistic or not, but his
attitude to his subject. That may be described as a
fixed resolve to omit nothing essential for the understanding of every side of the matter treated ; whereas
an idealistic art omits whatever for any reason, moral or
aesthetic, it may desire to disregard. But it does not
seem a very reprehensible thing to speak of the style
which naturally goes with realism as realistic ; and most
people do so quite happily. Where some err is in
taking 'realistic' as equivalent to 'vivid'. The
realistic style does tend to be vivid, although it does
not by any law of its being directly aim at vividness.
But what you find in practice is this. If the presentation of a mood or a landscape or a situation is complete
(which is what realism aims at), it will usually affect one
more powerfully and seem more vivid than a partial
presentation, however clear and bright. Then, to give
this completeness of impression, the style is forced
to employ concrete, familiar, sometimes ugly words ;
whereas idealism uses a selected vocabulary, which has
a tendency to become 'classical' or conventional.

Greek poetry is markedly idealistic, as indeed is

Greek art in general. Not that the Greek poets are afraid of saying anything, or rather of speaking quite frankly about anything—a real distinction, which certain modern writers are in the way of obliterating. They treat of matters and situations which we scarcely venture to discuss at all, and they do it without either prudery or brutality. How they do it is their secret. The question suggests itself whether this is not rather realism than idealistic art. It is however a mistaken question, because it reposes on the false assumption that idealism necessarily misrepresents the truth. No Greek would have accepted that; he was much more likely to make the contrary assumption. What is certain (and it is the point with which we are here concerned) is that Greek poetry does somehow succeed in giving us the strongest impression of truth and reality by a method that often seems positively to approach unreality. Great art always mocks our distinctions; it resolves contradictions in itself; it is alike classical and romantic, idealistic and realistic. But, remembering this, we may still say that Greek art followed the road of idealism to the point where it meets the other road.

Read the description of a fight in Homer, and then read one in Walter Scott or William Morris. You can hardly visualize Homer's fighting at all. To this day scholars cannot agree whether the warriors of the *Iliad* carried big oblong shields or smaller round ones, whether their swords were of bronze or iron. Homer appears to say now one thing and now the other, as if he did not know or care. Half the *Odyssey* is concerned with the adventures of Odysseus in Ithaca, and it is impossible to identify a single site described in the poem. The whole

Iliad (a much longer poem than the *Odyssey*) is about the War for Troy; yet Homer's topography is at best exceedingly vague, and at worst definitely mistaken. How comes it then that his poetry is so vivid? The answer to that is only arrived at when we have grasped the nature of the epic style. That conventional style does not concern itself with topography or local colour or anything except the particular effect it aims at producing, which is not so much a sense of verisimilitude in details (which the Greeks rather despised) as a sense of the heroic; and by the 'heroic' I mean what has a superhuman energy or vitality. Everything in Homer is sacrificed to this. All the glory and all the tragedy of war are uttered in him as nowhere else. But the unheroic side of it is unrepresented. The passionate wills of his people! I do not know of anything like it except perhaps in Balzac. And Balzac cannot give their burning words.

The descriptions in Homer are wonderful for their truth and vividness so far as they go; but they touch certain aspects only. And even in the use of description he follows a very marked convention. His best work in this kind is found in the similes; I wonder for what reason. He will say perhaps that the Myrmidons attacked like wolves, and give us the most brilliant little picture of a pack of wolves lapping the black water with their thin red tongues. But the effect of it is chiefly to lead our minds away from the Myrmidons to the wolves, and it is only by an effort that we bring them back. We do not feel that we understand the manner of the Myrmidons' fighting any better for the simile. And in fact the poet does not want us to do so. What he desires to produce is an impression of violence and struggle and lithe contending bodies, and so he brings in the wolves. He is full of 'the glory and bloom of the world'. He fills the mind with images of heroes and gods in battle, of boars and lions fighting in mountain glens, of thunder and tempest and all splendid elemental things. It is part of his art to mix these images cunningly, lest the imagination get a little wearied of one sort (and for our imaginations there is perhaps too much lion: consider the eleventh book of the *Iliad*). But there is this other and profounder reason, that idealistic art dare not encourage the curiosity of the imagination too far, lest the whole world of that art's creation crumble before a sense of its unreality. For Homer's is an utterly conventional world, whatever archaeologists may say. Indeed it is the archaeologists themselves who have done most to prove it. Homer's is a world in which no ugliness exists, where the gods are men and the men are gods, where the customs and beliefs of ages are mixed up in a timeless confusion. It is true to its own conventions, which is the only kind of truth a work of art need have.

An idealistic art is selective, and therefore almost necessarily generalizing. Let Homer describe a lion, and this is what he says:

'Hector retreated, turning, and going, and turning again like a bearded lion that dogs and men drive away with spears and with shouting from a cattle-stead; whose brave heart swells in his breast, and reluctant he draws back from the stalls.'

And again, a few lines after:

'Over Patroclus Ajax stood like a lioness over her

cubs when hunters have met her in the jungle leading her young: she glares savagely, frowning till her brows hide her eyes.'

Here is Browning's lion :—

> *One's whole blood grew curdling and creepy*
> *To see the black mane, vast and heapy;*
> *The tail in the air stiff and straining,*
> *The wide eyes, nor waxing nor waning . . .*
> *And you saw by the flash on his forehead,*
> *By the hope in those eyes wide and steady,*
> *He was leagues in the desert already,*
> *Driving the flocks up the mountain,*
> *Or catlike couched hard by the fountain,*
> *To waylay the date-gathering negress.*
>
> > *. . . the lion*
> *Ne'er moved, kept his far-reaching eye on*
> *The palm-tree-edged desert-spring's sapphire*
> *And the musky oiled skin of the Kaffir. . . .*

That is a good lion. But it is not a whit more convincing than one of Homer's. There is a difference however. What Homer describes is any lion or lioness, a typical lion ; what Browning is describing is a particular beast, a lion who has almost a personality of his own. Ancient art is concerned with the type much more than modern poetry, which concentrates on the individual.

This characteristic of Greek poetry, its curiously aloof and almost abstract handling of poignant situations, is best exemplified in Attic Tragedy, the most important and representative expression of the Greek genius. By this treatment the situations lose none of their poignancy. They even gain in one kind of dramatic value by their isolation from the minor accidents of life. One listens to a few words, significant in the midst of silence. The speaking voices seem to have an added pathos and great new meanings, because they are felt as coming to us through spaces of an almost supernatural atmosphere. *Their voice is thin as voices from the grave*, and as disturbing. For Greek Tragedy remained to the end an act of religion, and treats its subjects accordingly in a religious, that is to say in a selective and idealistic, spirit.

When Antigone goes forth to her living tomb, this is how she speaks:

"Tomb, bridal chamber, eternal prison in the caverned rock, whither I go to find mine own, those many who have perished, and whom Persephone hath received among the dead! Last of all shall I pass thither, and far most miserably of all, before the term of my life is spent. But I cherish good hope that my coming will be welcome to my father, and pleasant to thee, my mother, and welcome, brother, to thee; for, when ye died, with mine own hands I washed and dressed you, and poured drink-offerings at your graves; and now, Polyneices, 'tis for tending thy corpse that I win such recompense as this." [1]

How all the horror of the situation—a young girl walled up alive in a charnel-house—has been subdued down to the shadow of some dreadful, yet heroic, destiny awaiting dimly somewhere in the background! The horror is not exactly evaded—Greek art would not do that—but it is transmuted. Contrast with this what Juliet says:

> *Shall I not then be stifled in the vault,*
> *To whose foul mouth no healthsome air breathes in,*
> *And there die strangled ere my Romeo comes?*
> *Or, if I live, is it not very like,*

---

[1] The translation is Jebb's. Yet even in him notice the traditional "'tis" of the classical translator.

The horrible conceit of death and night,
Together with the terror of the place,
As in a vault, an ancient receptacle,
Where for this many hundred years the bones
Of all my buried ancestors are pack'd;
Where bloody Tybalt, yet but green in earth,
Lies festering in his shroud;

and so on.   The difference of method is very striking.

This difference is everywhere apparent; but it is perhaps most surprising, when one comes to think of it, in the description of physical beauty.   Personal comeliness meant so much to the Greeks, influenced them so much more than ourselves, that we would on *a priori* grounds expect their literature to be full of it. The exact contrary is true; that is, in the great age, for I am not speaking of the *Scriptores Erotici*.   In Homer and the Tragic poets we find a multitude of women whom we feel to be beautiful, but whose beauty we take for granted.   It is not described.   A single, often conventional, epithet is all we get: ' white-armed ' or ' flower-faced ' or ' yellow-haired '.   For some reason it suffices.   It has often been remarked that Homer (for instance) nowhere describes Helen ; he describes her effect upon others, and that is twice as telling, since he enlists our imagination on his side.   So when Aeschylus has to speak of Helen in the *Agamemnon*, this is how he does it :

' So would I say there came to Troy a spirit of windless calm at the first, a peaceful carven thing of Wealth, the arrow of a soft look, a heart-breaking flower of Love.'

Is this a description?   Hardly, it will be admitted, in the modern sense.   Not thus would Chaucer or Spenser or Keats or Morris describe Helen of Troy.

The third point I would note is the greater *exuberance* or *expansiveness* of English poetry. The Greeks always thought of beauty as a measured thing ; we have almost adopted as our motto the maxim of Blake : *Exuberance is Beauty.* Our colder Northern blood is stimulated to indulgences in colour and emotion, which the susceptible and fastidious Greek temperament avoided with an instinctive dread. (It is curious to note how the Roman temperament, which was not susceptible nor fastidious, gradually overpowers the Hellenic influence on its best poetry until we get the heady perfumes, the gross horrors, the loud rhetoric of the Silver Age.) The problem of the Greek poet was how to make a few simple words so alive and crowded with meaning as to affect us more than if all were said as emphatically as possible. There is hardly any mere rhetoric in the Greek poets ; *their* motto is rather *Prends l'éloquence et tords-lui son cou.* Contrast the stately, almost ritualistic, curses of Oedipus with the cursing of Timon or Lear. Contrast the words of Cleon in the *Antigone* when he hears of his queen's death :

" Woe is me ! these things will fit no other man, that I may escape the charge. It was I, I who slew thee, woe is me ! it was I—my words are true. O servants, lead me with what speed ye may, lead me hence, me whose life is now a living death."

Contrast this with the outburst of Othello :

> *O cursed, cursed slave !—Whip me, ye devils,*
> *From the possession of this heavenly sight !*
> *Blow me about in winds ! roast me in sulphur !*
> *Wash me in steep-down gulfs of liquid fire !—*
> *O Desdemona ! Desdemona ! dead !*
> *O ! O ! O !*

This fullness of utterance, which Matthew Arnold remarked in Shakespeare and Keats, but which in fact is characteristically English, surely reaches its culmination in Swinburne. There occurs to me an instance of his method which has the advantage of adducing the Greek for comparison. Euripides has the phrase 'on waveless sands' for a level space on which horses were exercised. Swinburne says of the Roman arena

> *On sands by the storms never shaken,*
> *Nor wet from the washing of tides,*
> *Nor by foam of the waves overtaken,*
> *Nor winds that the thunder bestrides.*

The two methods are directly opposite. The English seeks to obtain by expansion and emphasis what the Greek obtains by concentration and suggestion. In English the meaning, so to speak, opens outward; in Greek it opens inward.

There are subjects which appear to us to cry aloud for protestation and emphasis, and especially the subject of love. It is not merely that this interest may be said to have swallowed up all others in modern poetry, but that we use a different kind of language concerning it. Greek poetry, mainly for reasons involved in its history—its early association with religion—accords love certainly less room and importance than it had in Greek life. The subject is not avoided. The lyric and elegiac poets, whose verses have so largely perished, and the later, Bucolic poets and contributors to the erotic section of the *Anthology*, were full of it; while even among the dramatists Euripides handled it rather frequently, the writers of the Middle and New Comedy constantly. But Greek love, at any rate between man and woman, was not often in our sense romantic. It is regularly treated as an appetite, a necessity, sometimes as a curse ; occasionally as a great inspiration ; rarely indeed as an experience desirable in itself. As is perhaps natural, the words used of it are brief and deprecating. They are so even in Sappho, though their passion is extreme. It is not, I think, till one reaches the *Pharmaceutriae* of Theocritus that one finds a great love poem in the modern sense. We may regret this and think that the Greeks lost an opportunity. On the other hand we are saved from a deal of sentimentality, which is the particular demon that lies in wait for the soul of the Romantic. The *amoureux transi*, a very common character in Greek literature after the classical period, is not found in that period at all. What Greek of the Great Age would say :

> *But if we had loved each other—O sweet,*
> *Had you felt lying under the palms of your feet*
> *The heart of my heart beating harder for pleasure*
> *To feel you tread it to dust and death?*

It is no doubt disconcerting for the translator to find so large a part of his vocabulary useless to express the ancient attitude to the matter with which modern literature is chiefly concerned.

Then there is the difference which Arnold called one between *sanity* and *caprice*. Arnold was recommending the Greek claim, and in the context there is no strong objection to this way of pointing the contrast he has in mind. Otherwise, and on a broader consideration, it is somewhat unfair. There is always a certain begging of the question in a word like 'sanity' in any case; what are the limits of sanity? There were important elements in Greek life which you can only defend by rejecting the restrictions of the current morality. There are in the Greek dramatists, especially Euripides, extremely skilful and unflinching studies of definitely morbid moods. No doubt Arnold is thinking more particularly of style; although he takes the view (which in effect was Aristotle's) that 'everything depends on the subject'. Even so, had he lived to read the *Persians* of Timotheus, he would have found one of the most eccentric styles in existence, which nevertheless was not a mere freak, but representative (if possibly with some exaggeration) of a whole class of ancient poetry. One wonders a little too whether this 'sanity' is not something of a shibboleth or (to put it more politely) a convention imposed upon us by the unconscious agency of the classics themselves. There does not seem to be any convincing reason why a sonnet on a lady's eyebrow, written in the most fantastically precious language, should not be as sane as a *tirade* on the Death of Ajax. At least you would not think of locking up a young man in love for reciting extravagant sonnets; but if he went about declaiming like Addison's Cato, I think you would. A better term for the purpose than 'sanity' would be the word the Greeks themselves used, Sôphrosyné, which, applied to conduct, means 'self-control', and, applied to literature, might be taken to mean a moderate, restrained, not emptily conventional way of expression—a sort of good manners in style. Such a style avoids eccentricity, mannerism, and violence. It aims at setting up a standard. So far as this standard comes to be accepted by the average educated man, it becomes a canon of sanity' in contrast with the divagations of the literary heretic; *securus iudicat orbis terrarum.* In this sense Greek literature unquestionably possesses sanity, for none has had anything like the same success in imposing its standards upon others.

Essentially, Arnold is quite right. Greek literature is markedly free from caprice, from the stressing of the personal note. A more individualistic form of society has produced among us a more individualistic type of character. The doctrine has grown up that art is a medium for the expression of the artist's idiosyncrasy. A poet or a painter now speaks about '*my* art'. The ancient conception of the artist as one who says what the Lord puts in his mouth, or at least voices the general sentiment, has disappeared ; it may return. Meanwhile the chances are against it, at any rate in England. The English imagination is curiously self-willed and, as a consequence perhaps, self-analysing.

We have poets like Donne and Blake and Browning whose whole inspiration comes from the pursuit of beauty down byways. No Greek could possibly have written like any of them. These were of course exceptional men ; but only in the sense that they accentuate a definite bias of the English genius. Imagine what an Elizabethan dramatist (other than Shakespeare) would have made of a subject like almost any of those treated by the Attic tragedians. Think what Webster would have made of the murder of Clytemnestra, or Marston of the sin of Oedipus. Not merely would every dreadful circumstance have been dwelt upon, but all would have been done in the passionate egotism of the Elizabethan style, with the violent colours and exasperated rhetoric which somehow do achieve wonderful effects of power and beauty, but are anything rather than Greek. The classical effort in the eighteenth century did succeed in building up a sort of common form in style, but not in thought, which is the true basis of style; hence the tendency to an artificial diction, which again is anything but Greek. Now English poetry appears to be concentrating more and more on the search for novelty. The novelty may be of subject or of expression, or (of course) of both. If we choose to write about a very modern thing, like aeroplanes, we can afford to be simple and direct in style. If we write concerning love or death, we are very conscious of our predecessors and aim at saying something new and unexpected, or at any rate at saying the old things in a new and unexpected way. Or we may be Futurists or the like, and aim at combining both novelties. But the ancient view was that, when once a sentiment had been expressed as well as was necessary, the thing to do when you wanted it was to copy it out. . . .

It would be interesting to discuss the reasons for this. Some are historical and some psychological. I will here mention only one, and the reader may be disposed to regard it as fanciful. I think this restless search for new and striking effects is stimulated by an undefined consciousness of something that poetry has lost. Everyone remembers the saying of Bacon about the necessity of strangeness as an element in Beauty. This has been thought to represent the romantic point of view in contrast with the classical.

But Greek poetry is not without this quality of strangeness, although the strangeness comes to it in a different way than to ours. We remember that far the most important and representative kinds of Greek poetry—the Epic, the Drama, Choral Lyric—were composed for solemn occasions, as parts, we might venture to say, of a great and magnificent ritual. So, partly by aid of its surroundings, partly by attuning its language to these, Greek poetry concentrated upon itself a religious light, which naturally has a strange, impressive, supernatural quality. Any sensitive reading of a Greek tragedy will reveal this at once. We have to do without these aids, without the spiritual pressure of a great occasion to inspire the poet and urge the audience to seek deep meanings in old, simple, consecrated words. The modern poet, thrown upon his own resources, must produce all his magic himself. So he seeks to intrigue or stimulate the imaginations of his readers by the intensity or curiosity or suggestiveness of his language.

This is how William Morris speaks of death :

> *"Listen, suppose your time were come to die,*
> *And you were quite alone and very weak;*
> *Yea, laid a-dying while very mightily*
>
> *" The wind was ruffling up the narrow streak*
> *Of river through your broad lands running well:*
> *Suppose a hush should come, then some one speak:*
>
> *"'One of these cloths is heaven, and one is hell,*
> *Now choose one cloth for ever, which they be,*
> *I will not tell you, you must somehow tell*
>
> *"'Of your own strength and mightiness; here, see!'*
> *Yea, yea, my lord, and you to ope your eyes,*
> *At foot of your familiar bed to see*

" A great God's angel standing, with such dyes,
Not known on earth, on his great wings, and hands,
Held out two ways, light from the inner skies

" Showing him well, and making his commands
Seem to be God's commands, moreover too,
Holding within his hands the cloths on wands;

" And one of these strange choosing cloths was blue,
Wavy and long, and one cut short and red;
No man could tell the better of the two.

" After a shivering half-hour you said
' God help ! heaven's colour, the blue'; and he said, ' hell'.
Perhaps you then would roll upon your bed,

" And cry to all good men who loved you well,
' Ah Christ ! if only I had known, known, known;'"

One may take the wonderful speech of Claudio in *Measure for Measure*, or any of the numberless meditations on death in Donne or Browning or Walt Whitman —or any other modern poet. Compared with words like theirs, the utterances of the Greek poets may seem at first strangely bald and, as it were, inarticulate. Let yourself be penetrated by them a little further, and you will find in them a curious thrill of sincerity and passion. "Praise not death to me", says the ghost of Achilles in Homer, "rather would I be the servant of a poor man with a little farm than king over all the perished dead". That is all, but in such a place from such a speaker it is enough. With this pregnant simplicity the Greek poets handle all the great commonplaces. There is an anonymous *skolion* or drinking song, which literally translated runs thus:

'O that I were a fair great golden jewel untouched of fire, and a beautiful chaste woman were wearing me !'

The love poetry of the Greeks is not their strong point, but I hope a man may be allowed to prefer the brevity of the *skolion* to the song in *The Miller's Daughter*:

> *And I would be the girdle*
> *About her dainty, dainty waist . . .*

What then is the translator to do? He is clearly forced to a compromise. His language, if it is to look like English poetry at all, will be fuller, more coloured, more personal in the turn of its expression, than the Greek. He cannot force his medium out of its natural bent. The more he succeeds in that attempt the more plainly his work will bear the aspect of a *tour de force*: as witness *Merope*. On the other hand it is the translator's business to reproduce as closely as may be the special flavour and distinction of his author. Unless he does that, he justifies the Italian proverb. He must give up a little to both claims. But it need not be anything essential. It is not even so much a compromise that is necessary as an adjustment of values.

Greek poetry (for to this vital point we must always return) is the product of a different tradition from ours, and has all the associations of its tradition. The translator must be steeped in that tradition and in these associations if he is to seize the values of the Greek poetical vocabulary. To do this he must be a scholar, and an accomplished one, as well as a poet. His version must produce upon the English reader the effect which the original has produced upon himself. This means, not simply the transference of certain words and idioms into a different language, but the adaptation of the old tradition to a new habit of thought, a new direction of taste. It is a desperately hard thing to do.

In the actual work of translation there are two dangers to be guarded against: overtranslation and undertranslation. Greek life and society being so different from modern, many things are mentioned in Greek literature which we take for granted, many omitted which for us require explanation. The emphasis upon things to us unessential is perfectly natural in the original and does not offend the reader, who in fact does not notice it. But repeat the emphasis in English, and the perspective at once goes all awry. All these insignificant details are dragged into a ridiculous prominence and distract our attention from the things that matter. So a man reading a word for word translation of the *Iliad* might carry away chiefly an impression of how people in Homer cook their beef. Here then lies an obvious danger of overtranslation. But the other peril of undertranslation is even more insidious. A simple little word may convey so much in the original, and translated directly into English may look quite wretchedly meaningless. It is in this task that the quality of the translator is most severely tested. He has to convey in English the full poetical virtue of the Greek. He must do it without reading into the original what is not there ; there must be no 'added beauties' of his own. If he succeeds, he has a right to be impatient with the pedantry which requires him to do it in some way not his own. A man cannot write poetry in somebody else's way, and least of all in the pedant's.

A NOTE ON AUTHORITIES

I HAVE thought it inadvisable in a book like this to encumber the pages with references. But, as some readers will desire to examine for themselves the evidence on which I base some of my conclusions, I will here set down a selected part of it, with a brief bibliography, as relevant as I can make it.

For convenience of reference I number the Essays in Roman numerals, thus: I, II, etc.

I. I am greatly indebted to two pieces of writing by Prof. J. L. Myres: an article in the *Geographical Journal*, 1896, p. 605 ff., 'Maps used by Herodotus', and his Lecture on Herodotus in *Anthropology and the Classics* (Oxford). H. F. Tozer's *History of Ancient Geography*, 1897, is a useful book. There is a concise Appendix on the geography of Herodotus in How and Wells' *Commentary on Herodotus*, vol. I (Oxford).

P. 2 f. Herod. V. 49–51.

P. 4. Ar. *Clouds*, 200 ff.

καὶ τόδε Δημοδόκου· Μιλήσιοι ἀξύνετοι μέν οὔκ εἰσιν, δρῶσιν δ' οἷάπερ ἀξύνετοι.

P. 5. Herod. V. 52 f. II. 21, 23. IV. 8, 36.

P. 7. Herod. I. 171.

P. 8. Herod. IV. 145 ff.

The foundation of the Delphian Oracle is related in the Homeric (Pythian) *Hymn to Apollo*.

Fick, *Vorgriech. Ortsnamen*, p. 25. K. Penka, *Vorhellen. Bevölkerung Griechenlands* (Hildburghausen), p. 41. A. B. Cook, *Zeus* I. (Cambridge), p. 623 n. 6.

P. 9. For the Thalassocracy see discussions by Myres in the *Journal of Hellenic Studies* XXVI and XXVII, Fotheringham, *J. H. S.* XXVII, Murray in *The Rise of the Greek Epic*², 1911, Appendix C. Thuc. I. 4. Homer *Il.* II. 857.

P. 10 f. Herod. IV. 32–36. Paus. I. 31, 2. Pind. *Pyth.* X. 46 f.

P. 12. Herod. IV. 13–15. That the Hyperboreans originally sent their offerings to Artemis is a suggestion for which I am indebted to Mr. A. B. Cook.

The *Heracleia* is analysed by P. Friedländer in his *Herakles* (Berlin), 1907.

P. 16 f. *Cf. e.g.* IV. 195, 2. τὰ δὲ λέγεται γράφω· εἴη δ' ἂν πᾶν and VII. 152, 3, ἐγὼ δὲ ὀφείλω λέγειν τὰ λεγόμενα, πείθεσθαί γε μὲν οὐ παντάπασιν ὀφείλω.

P. 17. Herod. II. 32 f. IV. 191.

II. In writing on Thucydides I found especially helpful Prof. Bury's *The Ancient Greek Historians*, Lecture III (Macmillan), F. E. Cornford's *Thucydides Mythistoricus* (Ed. Arnold), and the relevant parts of Prof. Murray's *History of Ancient Greek Literature* (Heinemann) and Zimmern's *Greek Commonwealth*² (Oxford). An important book for English readers is Grundy's *Thucydides and his Age* (John Murray). Much interesting matter is found in Wilamowitz, *Aristoteles und Athen*.

P. 22 f. See *Thucyd. Mythist.*, Part II.

P. 25. Thuc. I. 70, 2 ff.

P. 26. II. 45, 4. The inscription is numbered CIA I. 433. The importance of the economic factor in Athenian history is well brought out by Mr. Grundy.

P. 28. II. 35–46. Soph. *Antig.* 332 ff.

P. 30. It was Prof. Murray who first compared Thucydides' 'virtue' with the *virtù* of Machiavelli. I. 22, 4. VII. 86. I. 9, 3. IV. 84, 2.

31 f. The Sophistic movement has been much written about. There is a vigorous defence of the Sophists in Grote's *Plato*, now somewhat antiquated. Gomperz, *Griechische Denker*, vol. I, and Prof. Burnet, *Early Greek Historians* [2] (A. and C. Black), *Greek Philosophy* I (Macmillan), may be consulted. The texts are collected by Ritter and Preller, *Historia Philosophiae Graecae*, etc.

P. 32. Herod. III. 38.

P. 36. The Plague II. 47–54.

P. 41. III. 37–40. On reading Cleon's speech over again, I am struck by a doctrinaire, almost pedantic, quality in it strangely mixing with its 'violence' and cruelty. It makes one think of Robespierre. Aristophanes of course is constantly attacking Cleon. The most sustained attack is in the *Knights*. It is far from a merely unqualified denunciation.

P. 42. μοχθηρὸν ἄνθρωπον VIII. 73, 3, *i.e.* Hyperbolus.

P. 43. For scandal about Pericles see Plutarch's *Life*.

P. 44. III. 82–84.

P. 45 f. Herod. I. 60.

III. I have drawn most from Hesiod's *Works and Days*, from Aristophanes, especially the *Peace*, the *Birds* and the *Acharnians*, and from Theocritus. But there is abundant material elsewhere: in Homer, the lyric poets, Xenophon, Longus, etc. Dion I have translated from the text of Wilamowitz in his *Lesebuch* II.

P. 52 f. A mass of fascinating lore about Arcadia is gathered in the 8th book of Pausanias (Translation and commentary by J. G. Frazer, *Macmillan*). Prof. Ridgeway thinks the Hind with Golden Horns was a reindeer. The Arcadians had their story about it in any case.

P. 54 f. Thuc. II. 17, 52.

P. 55. Black-figured vase in the Vatican. It is represented in Miss Harrison's *Themis* (Cambridge), p. 98.

For what follows to p. 68 I may give the following references: *Works and Days* (*passim*); Ar. *Acharnians* 241 ff. (Rural Dionysia), 995 ff., *Birds* 160 ff., 235 ff. (what birds eat), 469 ff. (birds older than gods), 710 ff., *Peace* 557 ff., 573 ff., 1127 ff. (praise of country life); Theocritus I. 15 ff., 21 ff., 46 ff., II. (*Pharmaceutriae*), V. 91 f., VI. 15 f., 39 f., VII. 14 ff., 22, 106 ff., 131 ff. (*Thalusia*), *ad fin.*

P. 59.   *Od.* XI. 489 ff.

P. 63.   See *Themis*, p. 419 ff.

P. 65.   Moschus, *Epit. Bion.* 106 ff.

P. 69.   See Prof. Phillimore, 'The Greek Romances' in *English Literature and the Classics* (Oxford).

IV. The most convenient summary of our knowledge concerning Demeter and Persephone is Farnell's *Cults of the Greek States*, vol. III. There is an enormous and highly controversial literature dealing with the Eleusinian Mysteries; but my little sketch does not involve itself in that. The reader will remember Pater's essay in *Greek Studies.*—The principal text is the Homeric *Hymn to Demeter*.

V. See Prof. Murray's Introduction to his translation of the *Alcestis* (Allen and Unwin). Compare what he says on the *Alcestis* in *Euripides and his Age* (Home University Series). There is a brilliant, if wilful, discussion of the play in Verrall's *Euripides, the Rationalist* (Macmillan).

P. 114 f.   *Bibl.* 1, 9, 15.

P. 115.   'Anodos Vases'. See J. E. Harrison, *Prolegomena* (Cambridge), p. 276 ff.

P. 116.   *Alc.* 444 ff.   834–836.

P. 117.   995 ff.   1020 ff.

P. 118. Anton. Lib. 23. My statement is perhaps too succinct. What Antoninus (quoting Hesiod and Nicander) says is αἱ δὲ—the cows of Apollo stolen by Hermes—ἐνέμοντο, ἵνα περ ἦσαν αἱ ʼΑδμήτου βόες. This for the mythologist amounts to identification, and the cows of Apollo are the same as 'the cows of Hades' (*Bibl.* 1, 5, 10). See *Themis*, p. 369 f. *Bibl.* 3, 10, 4, 1.

P. 119. Pind. *Frag.* 129 (Bergk). *Cf.* J. E. Harrison, 'Helios—Hades,' *Class. Rev.* XXII, p. 15.

P. 120. *Alc.* 746.

The explanation of Heracles as Leader of the Kômos is based on a mass of evidence which cannot even be summarized here. Neither is there anywhere anything like a complete statement and discussion of the vast Heracles-mythology. (Hercules is in much better case.) Preller, *Griech. Mythol.*, and Gruppe, *Griech. Mythol.*, give the most useful *compendia* of the facts. There are interesting discussions of Heracles' legend in K. O. Müller's *Dorians* I² and the *Herakles* of Wilamowitz, Part I. Heracles in art is treated in an important article by Furtwängler in Roscher's *Lexikon*.

P. 121. Kômos at Olympia : Frazer, *Golden Bough*³, III, p. 91. F. M. Cornford in *Themis*, ch. VII.

P. 122. καλλίνικος recurs in a significant way throughout Euripides' *Heracles*.

Pind. *Ol.* IX. 1 ff. with *schol.*

P. 123. Livy X. 23.

For representations of H. leading the Kômos see Furtwängler in Roscher. *Cf.* Ovid *Met.* IX. 271. Μουσαγέτης CIG 5987. *Cf.* 2214. Paus. IV. 31, 10.

The lyre-playing H. is a common art-type ; so is H. at the head of a joyous procession. How common the reader may see by running through M. Salomon Reinach's useful *Repertoires* of ancient art.

P. 124. *De restaur. schol.* 7. Suet. *Aug.* 29, etc. Ovid *Fasti* VI. 799 f.

For Athenian *thiasi* see Isaeus 9, 30.

Nillson, *Griech. Fest.*, p. 453.   Roscher's *Lex.*, p. 2947 f.

A. B. Cook, *Class. Rev.* XX, Nos. 7 and 8.

Diog. Laert. 6, 50.

P. 125.   Parasites of H.   Athen. VI. 26 (p. 234 E), 27 (p. 235 D).   Ritual cursing: *Bibl.* 2, 5, 11, 8.   Lactant *inst. div.* I. 21, 31.   H. ἀναπαυόμενος: Roscher, p. 2912 f.   *Cf.* Pind. *Nem.* I. 70.

P. 126.   H. as fertility-daimon: *Themis*, pp. 364–370.

H. and springs, etc.   Paus. I. 15, 3; 32, 6; II. 32, 4. *Cf.* Ἡράκλεια λουτρά.

Hermeraclas: Roscher, p. 2966.

With Eros: Paus. VIII. 31, 3.   *Themis*, p. 370 ff.

Μήλων: *J. H. S.* I. 1.   P. Gardner, *Types*, pl. 5, 2, 29.

H. as Dactyl: Paus. V. 7, 6; VIII. 31, 3; IX. 19, 4, 5. Strabo VIII. p. 355.   Diod. 64, 6.

C. Fries, *Studien zur Odyssee*, I (Leipzig), has much to say about triumphs.

128.   Pind. *Ol.* IX. 30 ff.   Roscher, p. 2186 f.

Paus. VIII. 31, 3; IX. 19, 5.

For what follows the reader may consult E. K. Chambers, *The Mediaeval Stage* (Oxford), and A. J. B. Wace, 'North Greek Festivals,' Brit. Sch. Ann. XVI, p. 232.

P. 130 f.   Arist. *Poet.* 1449ª.

P. 131.   Story of Omphale: *Themis*, p. 506.

P. 132.   Ar. *Wasps ad init.*, *Peace* 736.

P. 135.   This conjecture about the veil worn by Alcestis after her resurrection seems confirmed by the Oxford *Krater* (*J. H. S.* XXI, Pl. 1), on which Pandora, an Earth-Korê like Alcestis, wears a bridal veil.

P. 137.   Eur. *Alc.* 553 ff.

VI. P. 143, *Lectures on Translating Homer.*

P. 144.   *Il.* X. 137.   *Il.* XXI. 34 ff.

P. 147.   *Il.* XXIV. 543.   *Od.* VIII. 461 f.

Mr. Mackail in his *Lectures on Greek Poetry* (Longmans Green and Co.) dwells at some length on the quality of the simplicity in Greek poetry.

P. 149. Herod. I. 3.

P. 150. Herod. II. 120.

P. 151. Herod. II. 16. II. 143.

P. 152. Herod. III. 31. V. 80 f.

P. 153. Herod. VII. 45 f.

P. 155. See especially the *Frogs*.

P. 158. See my *Studies in the Odyssey* (Oxford), ch. IX.

P. 160. *Frogs* 340 ff.

P. 161. *Bacchae* 1005 ff.

P. 162. Pind. *Ol.* II. 91 f.

P. 163. See *Euripides and his Age* on the Chorus.

P. 169. Aesch. *Ag.* 958. *P.V.* 979 f. *Frag.* 161 (Nauck). Soph. *O. C.* 1549. *Frag.* 63 (Nauck). Eur. *El.* 900.

In the first quotation remark the peculiar value of κατασβέσει with its suggestion of 'quenching', which gives an image of the sea rising and raging like fire.

P. 170. Eur. *Frag.* 509 (Nauck).

Prof. Murray (Trans. *Alc.* p. 77) quotes *Alc.* 691 χαίρεις ὁρῶν φῶς, πατέρα δ᾽ οὐ χαίρειν δοκεῖς; as a line of the kind I have been quoting.

VII. The reader may consult Sellar, *Roman Poets of the Republic*[3] (Oxford), p. 280 ff., J. Masson, *Lucretius, Epicurean and Poet* (John Murray), and the commentary in Munro's great edition of Lucretius (Cambridge).

P. 183. *De R. N.* III. 933 ff.

P. 184. *De R. N.* III. 894 ff.

VIII. See F. Gummere, *The Beginnings of Poetry* (Macmillan); E. Grosse, *The Beginnings of Art* (Chicago); J. E.

Harrison, *Ancient Art and Ritual* (Home University Series).
G. Murray, *Hamlet and Orestes*, B. A. Shakespeare Lecture
1914, p. 23 ff., anticipates my conclusion.

P. 205.   *Il.* I. 267 ff.
P. 206.   *Themis* 112 f.

IX. P. 218.   Ag. 1146 ff.
P. 223.   *Il.* XVII. 108 ff., 133 ff.
P. 225.   Soph. *Ant.* 1317 ff.
P. 228.   Preface to 'Poems: A New Edition', 1853.
P. 236.   There are good remarks on this matter in the
Preface to *A Book of Greek Verse* by W. Headlam (Cambridge).

INDEX

UNWIN BROTHERS, LIMITED, THE GRESHAM PRESS, WOKING AND LONDON